Youth with Cancer

Facing the Shadows

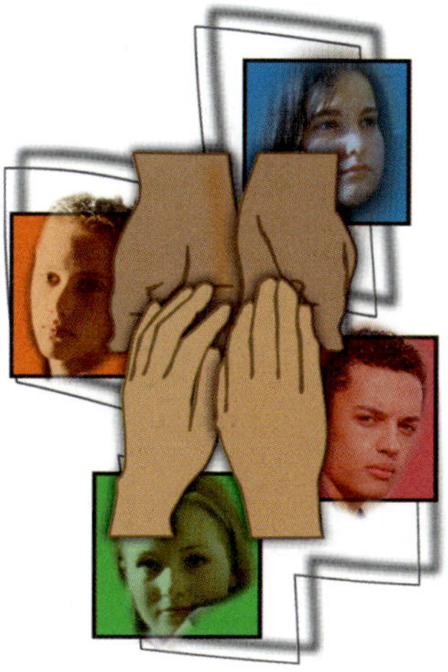

HELPING YOUTH WITH MENTAL, PHYSICAL, AND SOCIAL CHALLENGES

Title List

Youth Coping with Teen Pregnancy:
Growing Up Fast

Youth Who Are Gifted:
Integrating Talents and Intelligence

Youth with Aggression Issues:
Bullying and Violence

Youth with Alcohol and Drug Addiction:
Escape from Bondage

Youth with Asperger's Syndrome:
A Different Drummer

Youth with Bipolar Disorder: Achieving Stability

Youth with Cancer: Facing the Shadows

Youth with Conduct Disorder:
In Trouble with the World

Youth with Cultural/Language Differences:
Interpreting an Alien World

Youth with Depression and Anxiety:
Moods That Overwhelm

Youth with Eating Disorders:
When Food Is an Enemy

Youth with Gender Issues: Seeking an Identity

Youth with HIV/AIDS: Living with the Diagnosis

Youth with Impulse-Control Disorders:
On the Spur of the Moment

Youth with Juvenile Schizophrenia:
The Search for Reality

YOUTH WITH CANCER

Facing the Shadows

by Sheila Nelson and Ida Walker

Mason Crest Publishers
Philadelphia

Mason Crest Publishers Inc.
370 Reed Road
Broomall, Pennsylvania 19008
(866) MCP-BOOK (toll free)
www.masoncrest.com

First printing

1 2 3 4 5 6 7 8 9 10

ISBN 978-1-4222-0133-6 (series)

Library of Congress Cataloging-in-Publication Data

Nelson, Sheila.

Youth with cancer : facing the shadows / by Sheila Nelson and Ida Walker.

p. cm. — (Helping youth with mental, physical, and social challenges)

Includes bibliographical references and index.

ISBN-13: 978-1-4222-0139-8

1.Cancer in adolescence—Juvenile literature. I. Walker, Ida. II. Title.

RC281.C4N45 2008

616.99'400835—dc22

2006028798

Interior pages produced by
Harding House Publishing Service, Inc.
www.hardinghousepages.com

Interior design by MK Bassett-Harvey.
Cover design by MK Bassett-Harvey.
Cover Illustration by Keith Rosko.
Printed in the Hashemite Kingdom of Jordan.

The creators of this book have made every effort to provide accurate information, but it should not be used as a substitute for the help and services of trained professionals.

Contents

Introduction **6**
1. The Beginning **9**
2. Waiting to Hear **25**
3. Pickering **39**
4. Happy Birthday **51**
5. The Complications of Cancer **69**
6. Losing the Tumor **81**
7. Only the Good **97**
8. The Best Party **111**
Glossary **120**
Further Reading **122**
For More Information **123**
Bibliography **124**
Index **125**
Picture Credits **127**
Author and Consultant Biographies **128**

Introduction

We are all people first, before anything else. Our shared humanity is more important than the impressions we give to each other by how we look, how we learn, or how we act. Each of us is worthy simply because we are all part of the human race. Though we are all different in many ways, we can celebrate our differences as well as our similarities.

In this book series, you will read about many young people with various special needs that impact their lives in different ways. The disabilities are not *who* the people are, but the disabilities are an important characteristic of each person. When we recognize that we all have differing needs, we can grow toward greater awareness and tolerance of each other. Just as important, we can learn to accept our differences.

Not all young people with a disability are the same as the persons in the stories. But you will learn from these stories how a special need impacts a young person, as well as his or her family and friends. The story will help you understand differences better and appreciate how differences make us all stronger and better.

—*Cindy Croft, M.A.Ed.*

Did you know that as many as 8 percent of teens experience anxiety or depression, and as many as 70 to 90 percent will use substances such as alcohol or illicit drugs at some time? Other young people are living with life-threatening diseases including HIV infection and cancer, as well as chronic psychiatric conditions such as bipolar disease and schizophrenia. Still other teens have the challenge of being "different" from peers because they are intellectually gifted, are from another culture, or have trouble controlling their behavior or socializing with others. All youth with challenges experience additional stresses compared to their typical peers. The good news is that there are many resources and supports available to help these young people, as well as their friends and families.

The stories contained in each book of this series also contain factual information that will enhance your own understanding of the particular condition being presented. If you or someone you know is struggling with a similar condition or experience, this series can give you important information about where and how you can get help. After reading these stories, we hope that you will be more open to the differences you encounter in your peers and more willing to get to know others who are "different."

—*Carolyn Bridgemohan, M.D.*

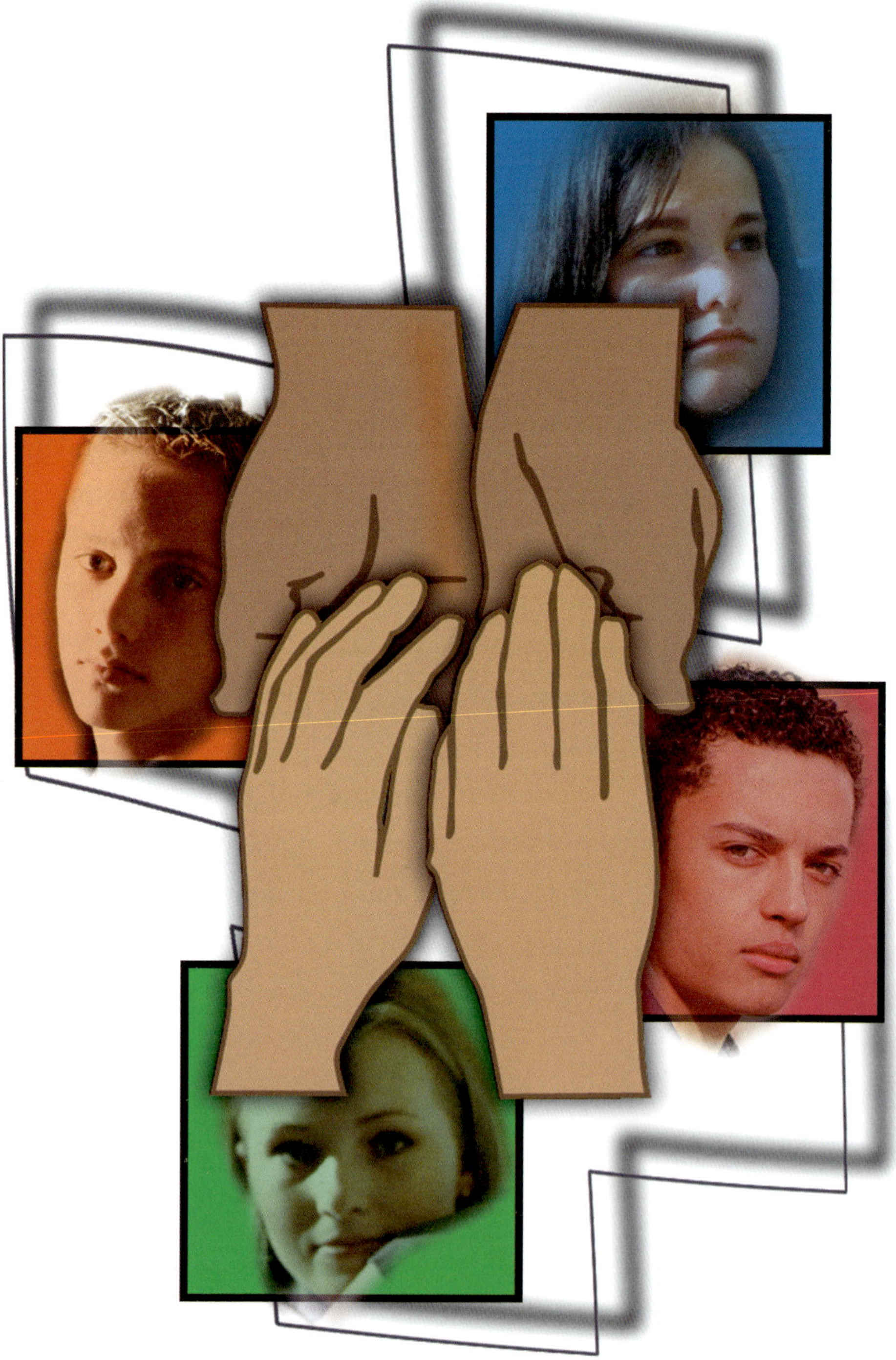

Chapter 1
The Beginning

"Pick up the pace, Hannah!" Mrs. Litsey called.

"Stupid gym class," Hannah muttered under her breath. Her left knee was throbbing, a dull ache that drowned out any thinking, and trying to run just made it worse. The cool autumn breeze lifted her thick brown curls away from her face and she glanced up. Most of the class had already rounded the far end of the track, and even the kids who were usually the slowest were ahead of her. She could see her friends Dani and Lauren in the middle of the group. They hadn't noticed when she had fallen behind.

The pain was starting to make her dizzy. She gave up and limped over to the bleachers.

"Are you okay?" Mrs. Litsey asked, coming over as Hannah sat down on the metal bench and put her head in her hands.

"My knee hurts." Hannah looked down at her leg. She couldn't see her knee under the gray sweatpants, but she imagined it purple and hideous.

"How long has it been hurting?" the teacher asked.

"I don't know. Maybe a couple of weeks." Hannah shrugged. The pain had eased a little when she sat down. "My mom said I had growing pains, but it's never hurt like this before."

Mrs. Litsey looked at her for a moment, frowning.

"I'm not faking," Hannah said. "Really!" She didn't like gym much, but she wouldn't have tried to pretend she was hurt just to get out of running.

"I know you're not," Mrs. Litsey said. "I think you should get checked out at the nurse's office. Do you need help to make it there?"

"Couldn't I just sit here for the rest of class?" Hannah asked. "Maybe it will get better."

"If it hurts so much you can't participate," Mrs. Litsey said, "it's bad enough for you to see the nurse."

"All right," Hannah agreed reluctantly, "but I don't need any help getting there."

Still, it took her ten minutes of slow limping to get to the nurse's office. When she slowed down enough, the pain was bearable. Whatever was wrong with her knee, she must have really messed it up when she ran on it in gym class. She hoped it would feel better by her birthday on Saturday. She was having a party, and not a kid party either, since she was going to be thirteen. Dani and Lauren and Becca and Jess were coming over, and some of her mother's students were going to give them manicures and fix their hair and makeup. (Her mother taught history, but Hannah guessed most college students knew a lot about hair and makeup.) Then her mother was going to take them to dinner at a nice restaurant and to a movie. Maddie and Isabel weren't going to come, since nothing ruined a good party like your annoying seventeen-year-old sister or your bratty nine-year-old sister.

Another boy was already in the nurse's office when Hannah arrived; he was pale and curled on a bed with his eyes closed. Great, Hannah thought, now I'll catch a nasty stomach bug or something on top of the knee thing.

The nurse came out of her private office when she saw Hannah through the glass window. She had long gray hair, and her expression was kinder than Hannah remembered from last year's vision and hearing screening. She pulled Hannah's chart, signed her hall pass, and had her sit on the other bed. Then she pulled a curtain, hiding the sick boy from view, and examined Hannah's knee, pushing up the leg of her sweatpants. The knee looked perfectly normal, not purple after all.

"It's a little swollen," the nurse said, feeling the knee gently. "Did you twist it, or fall on it?"

"No. I think it started hurting a week or two ago, but it's been getting worse, and today in gym it suddenly got really awful."

The nurse stood up. "Well, you definitely need to see a doctor. I can let you sign out some crutches for the rest of the day, but that won't fix the problem in the long run." She began to rummage in a closet for a pair of crutches the right size. "Why don't you sit there for a few minutes," she said over her shoulder. "I'll call your mother and see what she'd like you to do. If you start feeling better, you can probably go to your next class."

Hannah watched as the nurse went back into her office and picked up the phone. It was nearly ten-thirty Monday morning, and she wasn't sure whether her mother would be in class. The nurse was speaking, though; she paused, then nodded and said something else, so Hannah guessed she couldn't be just leaving a voice-mail message.

"Your mother is making a doctor's appointment for you," the nurse said when she returned. "She'll call back after she makes the arrangements. She said for you to go to class if you felt up to it, but if not, just to stay here." The nurse smiled. "She also said to tell you she loves you."

For the rest of the class period, Hannah sat on the bed and flipped through a magazine the nurse brought her. A few minutes before the bell rang, the nurse came out of her office and sat down on the bed next to Hannah. "Your mother called back and said you have an appointment this afternoon. She'll pick you up at two o'clock. Do you feel up to going to class until then?"

"Yeah, I guess so." Hannah wanted to change out of her gym clothes first, though.

"Do you think he's taking a long time?" Hannah asked her mother. It had been over two hours since they'd arrived at the pediatrician's office. Dr. Perillo, who had been her doctor since she was little, had looked at her knee and then sent her next door for X-rays. That had been almost an hour and a half ago. Now, Hannah and her mother sat in the waiting room, turning the pages of old magazines and watching a procession of kids and their parents come and go.

"He probably hasn't had a chance to look at the results yet," Hannah's mother said. "It's been pretty busy in here."

A nurse stepped into the waiting room and walked toward Hannah and her mother. "Mrs. Abrams?" the nurse asked. "Dr. Perillo would like to speak to you for a moment."

"What about me?" Hannah asked.

"Don't worry," her mother said, standing up. "Why don't you finish reading this article on herb gardens, so you can tell me what it says? I've always thought we should plant one someday."

Hannah felt a knot in her stomach as she watched her mother walk away with the nurse. What could Dr. Perillo want to say to her mother without her there? She tossed the magazine on the chair beside her without looking at it.

It seemed like another hour passed before her mother came back into the waiting room. Hannah, who was suspiciously analyzing her expression, thought she looked pale and serious, but she smiled at Hannah and motioned for her to follow her back into the doctor's office.

"Hello, Hannah," Dr. Perillo said. "Sorry for leaving you out there for so long. As I was just telling your mom, I was setting up some follow-up tests for tomorrow. I also want you to see an orthopedic specialist, a bone doctor."

"Why?" Hannah asked.

"Hannah, something showed up on the X-rays," her mother said gently.

"What kind of something?" Hannah could hear her voice shaking. She gripped her mother's hand.

"There's a tumor on the upper part of your left tibia, near your knee," Dr. Perillo said.

"A tumor?" Hannah's voice was a squeak. "You mean like cancer?"

Dr. Perillo smiled at Hannah reassuringly. "We won't know what kind of tumor until we do some more tests. There's also a hairline fracture in the same area, probably caused by the tumor pushing on the bone and weakening it. That would account for the pain you've been having today."

Hannah stared at him in disbelief. None of this made sense to her. It couldn't be right.

What Is Cancer?

Cancer is a scary word. Even today, with many treatment options available and **mortality** rates of many types of cancer dropping, the word "cancer" still conjures up fearful images and thoughts in many people. Well, what is cancer, anyway?

First, cancer is not just one disease. It is a group of more than one hundred different diseases. In each disease, something has happened to affect the life cycle of the cell.

The body is made up of cells. In a normally functioning body, cells grow, divide and create new cells, and then die. In the group of diseases called cancer, something happens to the **DNA** of cells in the affected area. They continue to grow and replicate uncontrollably; they do not die.

Affected cells may clump together to form masses called tumors. Some tumors are **benign**; these tumors are not life threatening. Others, however, are malignant—cancerous. Cells in malignant tumors will continue their uncontrollable growth and reproduction. Parts of the tumors can break off and use the bloodstream as a pathway to other parts of the body, spreading the cancer to other tissues and organs. When this happens, the cancer is said to have metastisized.

Who Gets Cancer?

People who get cancer come from all cultures, all races, all **socioeconomic** groups. However, some races are less prone to some forms of cancer than others. As with many illnesses, why someone develops cancer

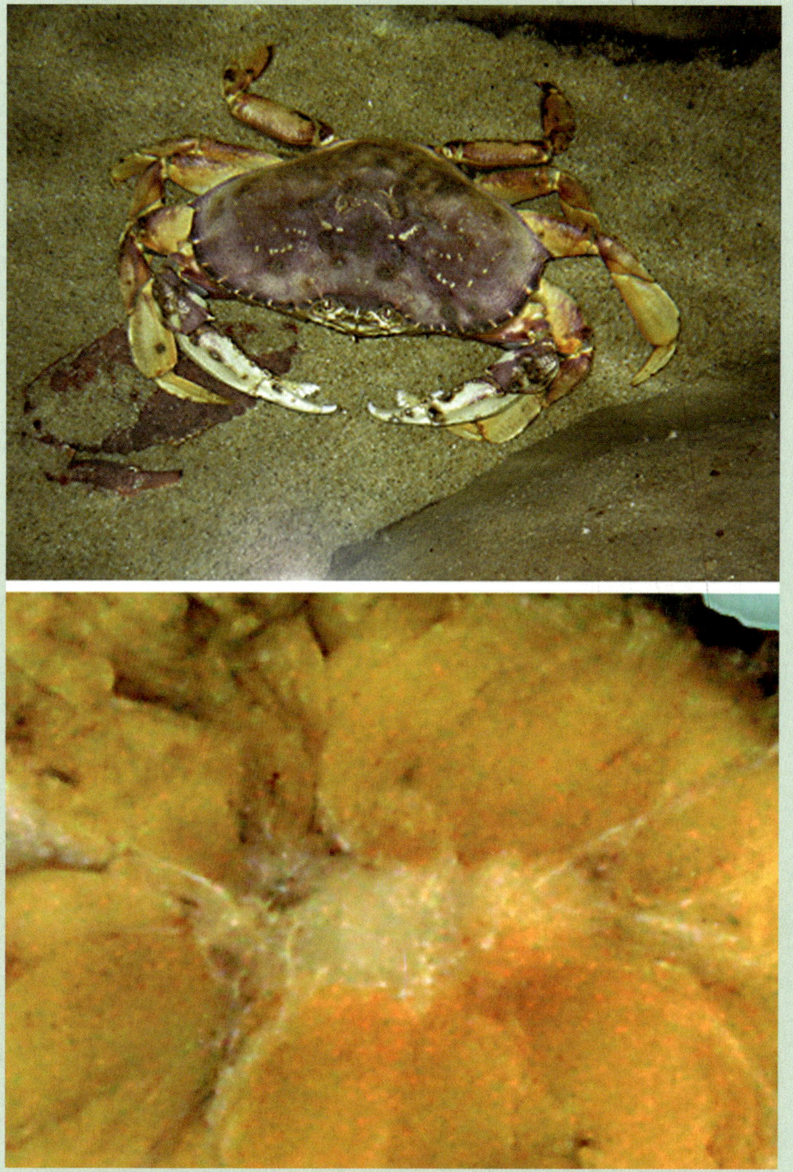

Cancer is the Latin word for crab. The name perhaps refers to the "crab-like" appearance of the cut surface of malignant tumors, which have a hard, roundish center surrounded by sharp projections.

and someone else doesn't is one of the unknowns. However, research has learned some things about what causes cancer and who is more inclined to get it.

As mentioned earlier, changes in the cell DNA affecting the cells' life cycle cause cancer. Not all causes for these changes are known, but some research indicates that **genetics**, lifestyle choices, and environmental factors can influence whether these genes will change.

Though cancer isn't inherited, many researchers believe that the **predisposition** to get cancer might be. This is often seen in breast cancer and colon cancer; if a close blood relative develops these cancers, one's tendency to get them might be increased. This isn't a "given," however. Simply having genes that are predisposed to becoming cancerous isn't enough to develop the disease. In many cases, it takes a **catalyst** for the cancer to develop.

People are responsible for their own behaviors and the consequences of those behaviors. One of those consequences could be cancer. For example, people who smoke cigarettes are more likely to develop cancers of the lung, throat, and mouth than are those who do not smoke. Those who spend time outdoors or on tanning beds without using sunscreen are more likely to develop one of the skin cancers than are people who do not spend a lot of time in the sun or who use appropriate sunscreen when they do. Again, these are not absolutes; participation in these activities simply increases the *possibility* that these cancers will develop at some point during one's lifetime.

Cancer is the result of changes to the DNA of cells in an affected individual. The altered DNA causes cells to grow and replicate uncontrollably, resulting in tumors.

People who smoke cigarettes are more likely to develop cancer of the mouth, throat, and lungs. These effects may not be seen for years, so that one who smoked as a teenager may develop cancer as an adult.

Diet can also influence who gets cancer, and a diet lower in fat and higher in fiber, fruits, and vegetables may help prevent cancers such as colon cancer. Some studies have shown that diet choices can even overcome what might seem to be a genetic influence on *not* developing cancer. For example, when living in Japan, Japanese women are less likely to develop breast cancer than are American women living in the United States. The reasons for this are not entirely known, but many scientists attribute the lower cancer rate to the Japanese diet. The average Japanese diet consists of very low fat intake and a diet high in fish rather than in the red meat Americans tend to consume. If a Japanese woman comes to the United States and assumes an American lifestyle and high-fat diet, however, her chances of getting breast cancer increase until it is almost the same as that of an American woman.

Cancers caused by tobacco and exposure to the sun or tanning beds do not develop right away. There can be many years between exposure and the appearance of cancer. Teens—and others, of course—must keep in mind that choices made now may have consequences many years in the future.

Researchers have begun studying the effect of the environment on cancer. On Long Island, New York, a breast **cancer cluster** was found, and in 1993, the Long Island Breast Cancer Study Project was established to determine if there was a link between cancer and environmental factors. In an area of upstate New York, research has been under way to see if the relatively high number of certain childhood and adult cancers can be traced to the dumping of chemicals into the soil. Other cancer studies focus on the use of aerosols and certain cleaning chemicals and their possible connections to the development of cancer.

Like the lifestyle influences on cancer, those forms of cancer caused by environmental factors do not occur overnight. There is much concern that children

Lifestyle choices influence an individual's chance of getting cancer. For example, a diet high in fiber, fruits, and vegetables may help prevent some types of cancer.

raised in environments where chemicals spilled or were dumped into the soil will develop cancer as adults. By that time, it may be difficult to trace the source of the cancer to a long-forgotten home.

Though it is still impossible to know with certainty who will develop cancer, it is a fact that increasing numbers of people are diagnosed each year with some form of cancer.

How to Reduce the Risk of Cancer

- Do not use tobacco products of any kind, including smokeless, "chewing" tobacco.
- Eat less fat and more vegetables, fruits, and whole grains.
- Exercise regularly and maintain a healthy weight for your height, gender, age, and activity level.
- Avoid the sun, especially when it is highest in the sky. Use sunscreen and wear protective clothing and a hat when going outside. If using a tanning bed, be sure to use sunscreen.

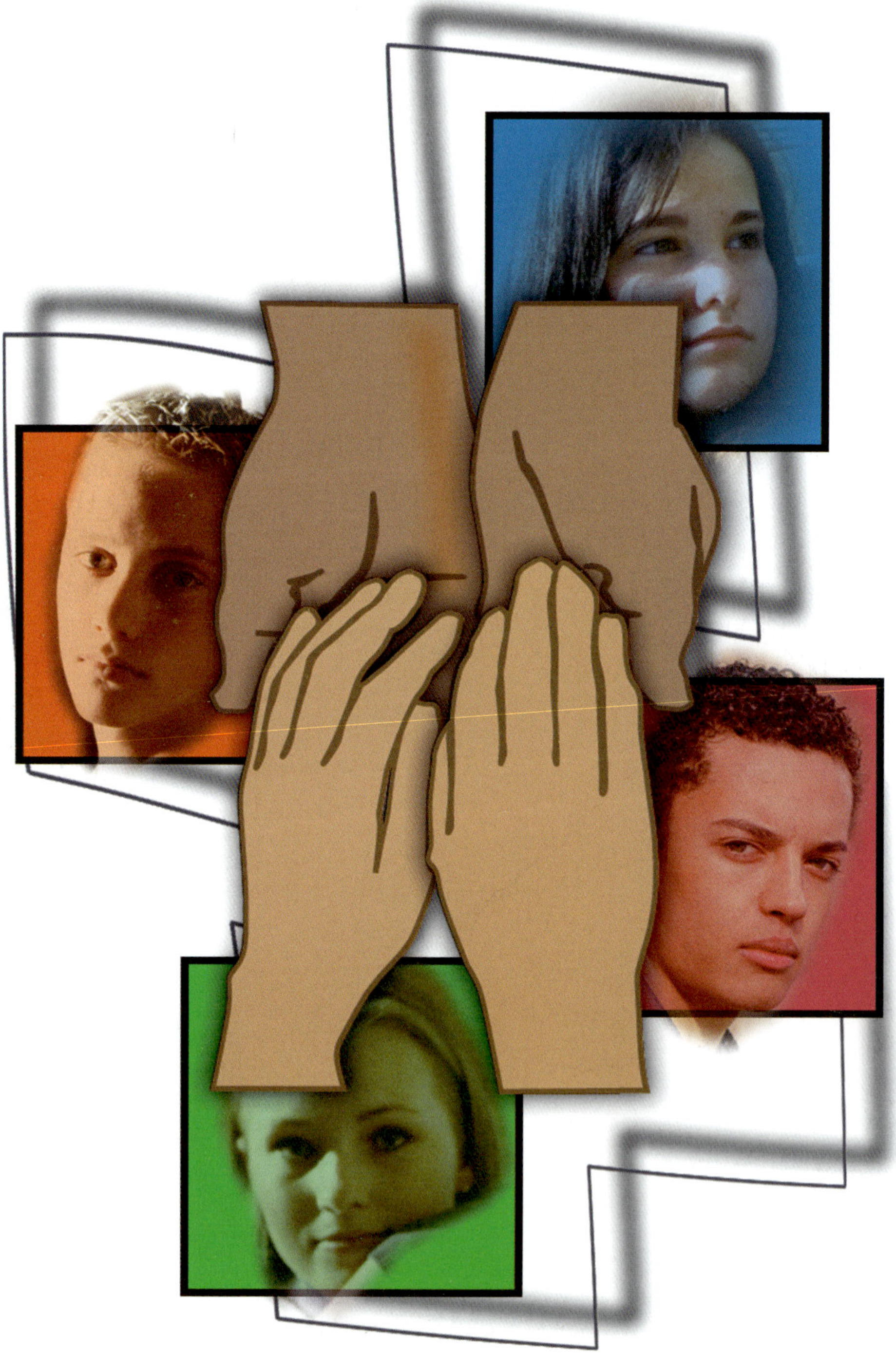

Chapter 2

Waiting to Hear

"Will the biopsy hurt?" Hannah asked. She lay on a hospital bed dressed in a blue and white gown. An IV needle dripped clear fluid into her arm. The medicine was making her drowsy, but it couldn't completely take away her fear.

"We'll numb the spot with a local anesthetic," the nurse said, "and the medicine in that IV will relax you, but you might feel a bit of pressure or a little pain. It shouldn't be too bad, though."

Hannah's mother, sitting beside her, squeezed her hand. "I'll be right here the whole time."

The doctor walked into the room and smiled at Hannah. He was young and good looking, and she smiled back.

"Good morning, Hannah," he said. "I'm Dr. Qazi. I know you're nervous, but we're going to try to make this as quick and painless as possible. I'm going to use a special needle to take a piece of the tumor out of your leg. Then I'll look at the cells under a microscope and see what's going on in there."

Back home that evening, Hannah stared at the tuna casserole on her plate, pushing the noodles around with her fork without eating. Dr. Qazi had said the results from the biopsy would take a couple of days, and she felt sick with worry.

After the biopsy, she had met Dr. Selkirk, the orthopedist. Dr. Selkirk was a tiny woman, with short curly red hair and a quick smile, and in other circumstances, Hannah would have liked her a lot.

"The tumor could be a couple of things," Dr. Selkirk had said. "If it's benign, we'll take it out and that will be that. If it isn't benign, we'll need to start a treatment plan to get rid of the cancer."

Cancer. Hannah hated that word.

"Why aren't you eating?" Isabel asked. "If I have to eat it, you have to eat it."

Hannah looked up from her plate. Her whole family was staring at her, her mother with sympathy, her older sister Maddie with curiosity, and Isabel with annoyance. Hannah glared at Isabel. "I'm not hungry. Shut up."

"Hannah," her mother said. "I know you aren't feeling well, but I still expect you to be polite. If you're not hungry, you don't need to eat, but I'm putting your plate in the fridge for when you do decide to eat."

"But you said I have to eat it now," Isabel objected. "That's not fair. Why doesn't Hannah."

"Life's not fair," Maddie said. "And what's wrong with my tuna casserole anyway?" On days when their mother had late classes, Maddie, and sometimes Hannah, made supper. Isabel helped out, but she had never cooked a full meal by herself yet.

"I hate fish, that's what's wrong with it!" Isabel said. "And I told you that, but you wouldn't listen to me."

Hannah listened to her sisters bicker. How could they sound so normal when her world felt as though it had just shifted, as if somehow she was teetering on the edge of a cliff? Their father had died of cancer, years ago when Isabel was just a baby. Isabel, with her straight dark hair and dark eyes, looked just like him, while she and Maddie looked more like their mother.

Suddenly, Hannah pushed back her chair and stood up. She grabbed her crutches and limped out of the room as quickly as she could, ignoring her mother when she called after her. She didn't want anyone to see the tears streaming down her face.

The next several days were agony. She knew her mother must have talked to Maddie and Isabel after she had left the table on Tuesday night, because they had started treating her differently. Maddie kept trying to be nice instead of bossy, while Isabel had gotten quiet and Hannah often caught her staring at her worriedly.

Hannah had tried to talk her mother into letting her stay home from school on Wednesday and Thursday, but her mother had insisted she go.

"School will help take your mind off things," her mother had said. "It will be good for you to be with your friends."

She had agreed to drive Hannah to school and pick her up afterward, though, so she wouldn't have to ride the bus with her crutches.

"Think positive," she had said as Hannah got out of the yellow SUV on Wednesday morning.

Positive. Sure.

The call came after supper on Thursday. Hannah was sitting at the kitchen table, trying to work on her social studies report on South Korea, but she was having trouble concentrating. Isabel sat across from her, doing math homework. She was smiling to herself, because Isabel loved math.

Hannah could hear Maddie typing at the computer in the living room.

When the phone rang, Hannah froze. "Oh, hi, Cara," she heard her mother say from her office down the hall, and Hannah relaxed. Aunt Cara was married to Uncle James, her mother's brother. She tried to eavesdrop on the conversation, but her mother closed her office door and she thought they were probably talking about her. Although maybe they were talking about her birthday and not her leg, she thought after a moment. *How's that for thinking positive?*

Twenty minutes later, Hannah had written only one sentence. *The country of South Korea is located on the southern part of a peninsula between China and Japan.* Across the table, Isabel was flying through her math problems.

The door of her mother's office opened, and her mother came down the hall into the kitchen. "Hannah," she said, "could I talk to you in my office?"

Hannah stared at her. She looked very serious. "Did the doctor call?" she asked, barely breathing. "Do I have cancer?"

In the living room, the sound of Maddie's typing stopped. Isabel looked up from her homework, her eyes huge.

Their mother sighed. "I wanted to talk to you alone first, Hannah," she said. "Yes, Dr. Perillo beeped in while I was talking to Aunt Cara. Dr. Qazi called him this evening with the biopsy results." She paused, and Hannah could see the answer in her face before she spoke again. "The tumor is cancerous, but the doctors are going to look after you and—"

Hannah interrupted, "No! That can't be right. Maybe they got the test results mixed up." This could not be happening.

Isabel started to cry. "Is Hannah going to die?"

"No, Hannah isn't going to die." Their mother sat down next to Hannah and hugged her. "Come here, Isabel," she said, and put one arm around Isabel when she came around the table to lean against her. Maddie came into the room silently and put her hand on Hannah's shoulder.

"But Daddy had cancer and he died," Isabel said, her face muffled against their mother's neck.

"Hannah isn't going to die," their mother repeated firmly. "You're going to go into the hospital tomorrow morning, Hannah, so the doctors can look after you better. We're going to get through this."

Hannah looked down at her leg. She listened to Isabel's stifled sobs and felt Maddie awkwardly rubbing her arm. Her body had betrayed her, making her sick from the inside out. She pressed her face into her mother's shoulder and started to cry.

Symptoms and Detection of Cancer

Individuals know their own bodies best. So, they are the ones to know when changes occur. But, what should one look for?

The key word is *changes*. Some common symptoms of cancer include:

- a *change* in a wart or mole
- a *change* in bowel or bladder habits
- a *change* in weight

The earlier cancer is caught, the better the chance of a successful recovery. Therefore, it is important to pay attention to warning signs, such as a sudden change in weight.

Benign tumors, infections, and other, non-cancer,illnesses can cause these and other cancer symptoms as well. Whenever someone notices one of these and other symptoms listed elsewhere, a visit to the doctor is called for. The earlier cancer is detected, the better the **prognosis**.

The doctor has many tools in her arsenal to use in the diagnosis of cancer—or to rule it out as a cause of the presenting symptoms. She may examine blood cells (remember, cancer is caused by a change in cells) to see if they are healthy and if there are enough of them.

Doctors can also use X-rays and magnetic resonance imaging (MRI) scans to find tumors. If a tumor is found, the doctor will decide if it is best to wait a few weeks or months to see if there are any changes, or if a biopsy should be performed immediately to find out if the tumor is cancerous. Sometimes the sample needed for a biopsy can be taken with the insertion of a long needle. Other times, the surface is scraped to obtain a cell sample or a small incision is made to remove tissue. However the sample is retrieved, a **pathologist** will study it under a microscope to determine if it is malignant or benign. If cancer is found, a treatment **protocol** can be started, and the sooner the treatment begins, the greater the possibility of beating the illness.

Common Symptoms of Cancer

- extreme exhaustion
- swelling or lumps in certain parts of the body, such as the abdomen or breast

- appearance of a new mole or a change in an existing wart or mole
- changing bowel or bladder habits
- loss of weight though not on a diet
- headaches
- blurred vision
- unusual bleeding
- problems with walking or balance

Remember, though, that the appearance of any of the above symptoms does *not* always mean you have cancer. Only a doctor can tell for sure.

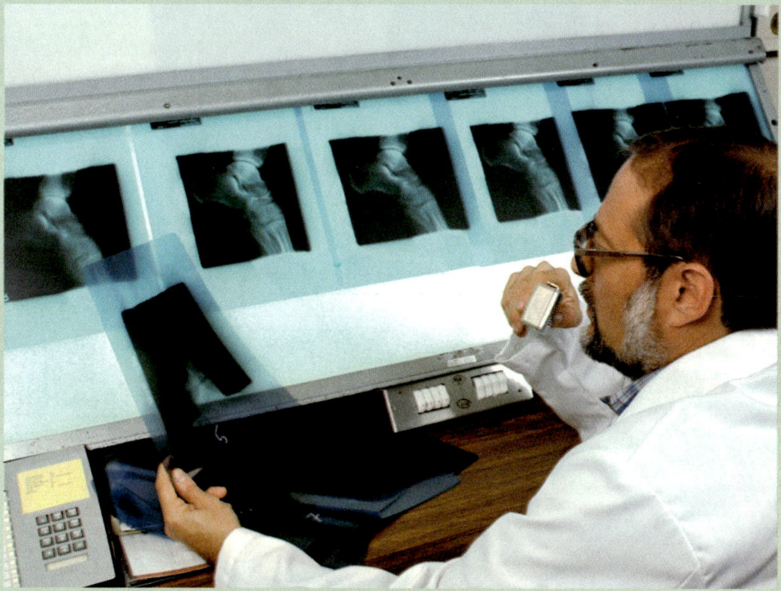

A doctor might use an x-ray to determine if a tumor is present. Once found, a biopsy is performed on the tumor to see if it is malignant or benign.

You cannot "catch" cancer by hanging out with a friend who has it. Rather, cancer is thought to be the result of interactions between genetics, environment, and lifestyle.

How Do You Get Cancer?

It was once believed that you could "catch" cancer. After someone died from the disease, it was not uncommon for the bed—including mattress and linens—and personal items such as clothing to be burned so as not to spread the disease.

Today, doctors know that cancer is not contagious; it cannot be spread from person to person. Instead, it is caused by a combination of genetic and environmental factors.

Cancer is never a person's fault.

Cosmetics and Cancer

One of the most anticipated crossroads for girls is when they are allowed to wear makeup. However, this transition may not be as harmless as most people think.

According to a December 2005 article in the *Palm Beach Post*, many products popular among teenage girls contain toluene and dibutyl phthalate, ingredients that have been linked to cancer and birth defects.

Does this mean someone should throw away her cosmetics and go around bare-faced? Not at all. Do your homework about the ingredients included in the products. Don't assume that just because products are available there are no potential problems with their use. Education is a wonderful—and effective—method of prevention.

Cancer Survival Rates

(in percentages, according to the Memorial Sloan-Kettering Cancer Center, www.mskcc.org.)

According to *Disease & Disorders*, more than 11,000 cases of cancer in young people are diagnosed each year. More and more people diagnosed with cancer are surviving, however. Take a look at the percentages in 2005 compared to those in 1962:

Type of Cancer	**1962**	**2005**
acute lymphocytic leukemia	4	75
acute myeloid leukemia	4	49
childhood leukemias (all types)	4	72
Ewing's sarcoma	5	58
Hodgkin's disease	50	90
neuroblastoma		
(non-stage 4)	10	85
(stage 4)		25
osteosarcoma	<20	63
retinoblastoma	75	94
Wilms' tumor	50	93

Fast Facts About Cancer

- In 2005, about 1.4 million new cases of cancer were diagnosed in the United States.
- In 2005, more than 550,000 people died from a form of cancer.

- Cancer is the second leading cause of death in the United States.
- About 64 percent of all people diagnosed with cancer will be alive five years after diagnosis.

Most experts consider someone cured of cancer if she has been cancer-free for five years. This does not mean that the cancer will not recur either in the same area or elsewhere.

Chapter 3

Pickering

Hannah's room on the pediatric oncology floor of Pickering Memorial Hospital had pale purple walls with a poster of a cheerful red lion on the wall opposite the bed. A recliner sat in one corner, and three straight-backed chairs stood against the walls, two on one side of the room and one on the other. Hannah sat on the edge of the bed and bounced a little, feeling strange and depressed. Her mother, Maddie, and Isabel had come with her because, as her mother said, they were all in this together. Maddie was carrying Hannah's pink overnight bag, while Isabel lugged Hannah's backpack full of schoolbooks.

The nurse who had led them to the room pointed to a cupboard next to the door. "While you're here, you can wear your own clothes as much as you'd like, but there are hospital pajamas and T-shirts in here if you want them," she said. "Dr. Stratton is planning on meeting with you at ten, but before he gets here we're going to take a few vials of blood. I'll be back to do that in a few minutes, so just get comfortable on the bed."

They were all quiet for a moment after the nurse had walked out of the room. "I brought some cards," Maddie said finally. "Does anyone want to play rummy?"

When the doctor arrived half an hour later, Hannah was sitting on the bed with her good leg curled under her and her sore one stretched out. A bandage on the inside of her right elbow covered the spot where the nurse had drawn blood. Isabel sat on the end of the bed, and Maddie and her mother had pulled chairs over.

"Who's winning?" the doctor asked. He was tall, with short dark hair and a neat dark beard.

"Maddie," Hannah said, pointing at her older sister.

"She always wins," Isabel added with disgust.

The doctor laughed and pulled the third chair away from the wall. He turned it around and sat on it backward, resting his arms on its back. "I'm Alex Stratton. I'm going to be your primary oncologist. That means I'm going to be coordinating your treatment, but a lot of people are going to be working together to make sure you get better. Now," he said, "you're Maddie, and I'm guessing you're Hannah." He nodded at Maddie and then Hannah. "So what is your name?" he asked, turning to Isabel.

"Isabel."

"Jena Abrams," Hannah's mother said when Dr. Stratton looked at her. She got up and leaned across the bed to shake his hand.

"I'm glad you came with Hannah today," Dr. Stratton said, looking at Maddie and Isabel, "because it's important that you all understand what's happening with Hannah's treatment. Yes, Hannah is the one with cancer. She's the one who will be getting a lot of nasty drugs to shrink the tumor in her knee, and she's the one who gets to stay in the hospital for a few days." He smiled at Hannah. "But cancer happens to the whole family. Your lives will be changing too. It might seem like Hannah is getting more attention and that you all have to give up things, and it's perfectly normal if you get angry about that sometimes. For example, I notice you've all given up school for today to be here." He wiggled his eyebrows and Isabel giggled.

"Are you going to tell me why this happened?" Hannah interrupted.

Dr. Stratton let out his breath in a small laugh. "I wish I could," he said. "If doctors knew why cancer happened we would be able to help prevent it. We do know about some kinds of cancer, like we know that smoking increases the risk of lung cancer, but those are mostly cancers that adults usually get. The cancers more common in kids and teenagers are different than the common adult cancers.

"You have a kind of cancer called osteosarcoma. Cancer happens when something goes wrong with a cell—in your case a bone cell—and it gets out of control, dividing and making new cells just like it, without the boundaries that keep normal cell division in check. The bone cells in your leg were working away, building new cells to help your legs get longer as you grew. All of your cells have instructions written inside them telling them when to divide and how to go about copying themselves. Then, one of your bone cells got the wrong instructions—and we don't know why that happened—which told it to divide and copy itself as quickly as it could. The result is that tumor at the end of your tibia."

"How big is it going to get?" Hannah asked. She pictured her knee swollen to the size of a basketball.

"It's not going to get any bigger if we can help it," Dr. Stratton said. "This evening you're going to start your first cycle of chemotherapy. The chemo drugs will kill the cancer cells and shrink the tumor. Your chemotherapy will be the first phase of your treatment, and it will probably last about three or four months. Then you'll have surgery to take out what's left of the tumor. After that, you will probably have a few more cycles of chemo, just to zap any cancer cells that break loose when we take out the tumor."

"Three or four months?" Hannah asked. "I'm going to be here that long?"

"You won't be here the whole time, but you will be in and out a lot. On the days you're having chemo treatments, you'll stay overnight here, but in between you can go home. Our goal is to have you here as little as possible." He smiled at her.

A knock sounded on the door, and Hannah looked up. A petite dark-haired woman stood in the doorway wearing a light blue hospital uniform.

"Oh, good," Dr. Stratton said, standing up. "Hannah, this is Mandy Wickstrom. She's an oncology nurse, and she will be overseeing the hands-on aspects of your treatments. I'll be checking in on you from time to time, and, of course, you can talk to me about any questions you have, but Mandy will be the one you see most often. I'll leave you to talk with her now about what's going to happen today. Don't worry, Hannah, we're going to take good care of you." He smiled again and left the room.

"Hello, Hannah," the nurse said in a chirpy voice, after the doctor had gone. "You can call me Mandy too, if you want. Later this afternoon you are going to have a small surgery to insert a Broviac catheter into your chest. That will act as a permanent line while you are getting your chemo over the next few months. Then, this evening, you'll get your first chemotherapy treatment. Tomorrow, you'll have another one, and then you can go home for a few weeks. These first two days you will have an infusion of cisplatin and doxorubicin. Later on in the chemo cycle, you will be coming back for several infusions of methotrexate. Do you have any questions?"

She had been talking quickly, and Hannah felt almost dizzy. She wasn't sure she'd understood anything the woman had said. "Surgery?" she asked. "But Dr. Stratton said I wouldn't have surgery for at least three months."

"That would be for your knee," Mandy said, speaking more slowly this time. "Today's surgery is to put in a central line, a Broviac catheter. You will get your chemo drugs through the Broviac, instead of through an IV. We would have to put the IV in every time you came to the hospital for a treatment, and that could mess up the veins in your arms. The Broviac will deliver the medicines directly into a major blood vessel near your heart."

Mandy looked at Hannah's face. "I know this is a difficult time for you, but remember, positive thinking is very important. Keep smiling! We must keep our spirits up!" She smiled brightly. "I must be off, but you can push that button to call the nurse if you need anything."

"I don't like her," Hannah said, after Mandy had gone. "We must keep our spirits up," she mimicked.

"I'm sure she means well," Hannah's mother began, and then stopped. "You don't have to like her, Hannah."

The idea of an unexpected surgery had upset Hannah, and she was even less happy when a nurse informed her that it meant she wouldn't be eating lunch. Not that she really felt like eating much, but having the option would have been nice.

She didn't want to think about the surgery. She didn't want to think about what chemotherapy might feel like, the idea of poisons pumping through her body. How were the chemo drugs supposed to know which cells were cancer and which weren't, anyway?

The Treatment Team

If test results are positive for malignancy, an entire team of treatment professionals spring into action. Many, such as attending physicians, radiologists, psychiatrists, and staff nurses, are common to other medical illnesses. There is, however, a group of medical professionals dedicated to **oncology**.

The Medical Team

The *primary oncologist* is the doctor in charge of cancer treatment. Oncologists are medical doctors who have specialized in treating cancer. The primary oncologist oversees treatment and communicates with the individual's primary-care physician.

Many forms of cancer respond well to radiation treatments. A *radiation oncologist* is a doctor with special training in the use of radiation in treating cancer.

An *oncology fellow* is a doctor who has completed her **residency**. As an oncology fellow, she will receive extra training to become an oncologist. The oncology fellow *is* a fully certified physician.

Surgeons are members of the treatment team for many medical conditions. Because surgery is often a recommended treatment method for cancer, they are integral to the cancer treatment team. A *general surgeon* may be called in to insert a **catheter**. If bone cancer is diagnosed, the skill of an *orthopedic surgeon* will be required. *Neurosurgeons* are called on to perform surgery on the brain and spine, such as the removal of a brain tumor.

People hospitalized for cancer treatment may be under the care of an *oncology nurse*. This nurse is generally a licensed *nurse practitioner* (NP) or *advanced practice nurse* (APN) with specialized training in the treatment of cancer. An NP or APN has received additional training beyond that of registered nurses or practical nurses. These nurses are equipped to perform patient physicals, make some diagnoses, and order lab tests. In many hospitals, people being treated for cancer will be seen by an NP or APN more often than by their physicians. The NP/APN, like all

Cancer is not a simple diagnosis. As a result, treatment will require a team made up of doctors, nurses, surgeons, and non-medical personnel, each playing a unique and vital role.

members of the treatment team, works closely with the primary oncologist.

Nonmedical Members of the Treatment Team

Someone being treated for cancer has many needs, and not all of them can be filled by medical personnel. An effective treatment team includes providers of nonmedical support as well.

Any **chronic** medical condition requires many adjustments by the person with the condition and family members. A *social worker* can help individuals learn to deal with the changes that the medical condition and treatment regimen require. Social workers are there to listen and to help. Sometimes that help just requires being there to listen about concerns, and other times it's helping individuals through the myriad red tape that might be involved in hospitalization and treatment.

A common side effect of a diagnosis of cancer and subsequent treatment is depression. The *clinical psychologist* is there to diagnose depression and other problems dealing with cancer. He can listen and help, or, if medication is required, inform the physician or refer the individual to a psychiatrist; in most states, psychologists cannot prescribe drugs.

Long or frequent hospitalizations are sometimes required for cancer treatment. A *child life specialist* is trained in child development and helps provide age-appropriate activities to help children and teens meet their social needs. In some hospitals, they also provide emotional support to patients going through difficult procedures.

Eating healthfully is important throughout life, but it is especially important for someone undergoing cancer treatment. Unfortunately, eating anything is often one of the last things an individual can think about at this time. A *registered dietician* has received training in nutrition for people with many medical conditions, including being treated for cancer. He can teach individuals and their families the best way to make certain the person in treatment receives all of the nutrients necessary.

Most health-care facilities have *chaplains* on staff to provide spiritual support to people in treatment and their families. In many, representatives from Protestant, Catholic, and Jewish faiths are readily available. They can also help individuals find clergy from other religions to provide support.

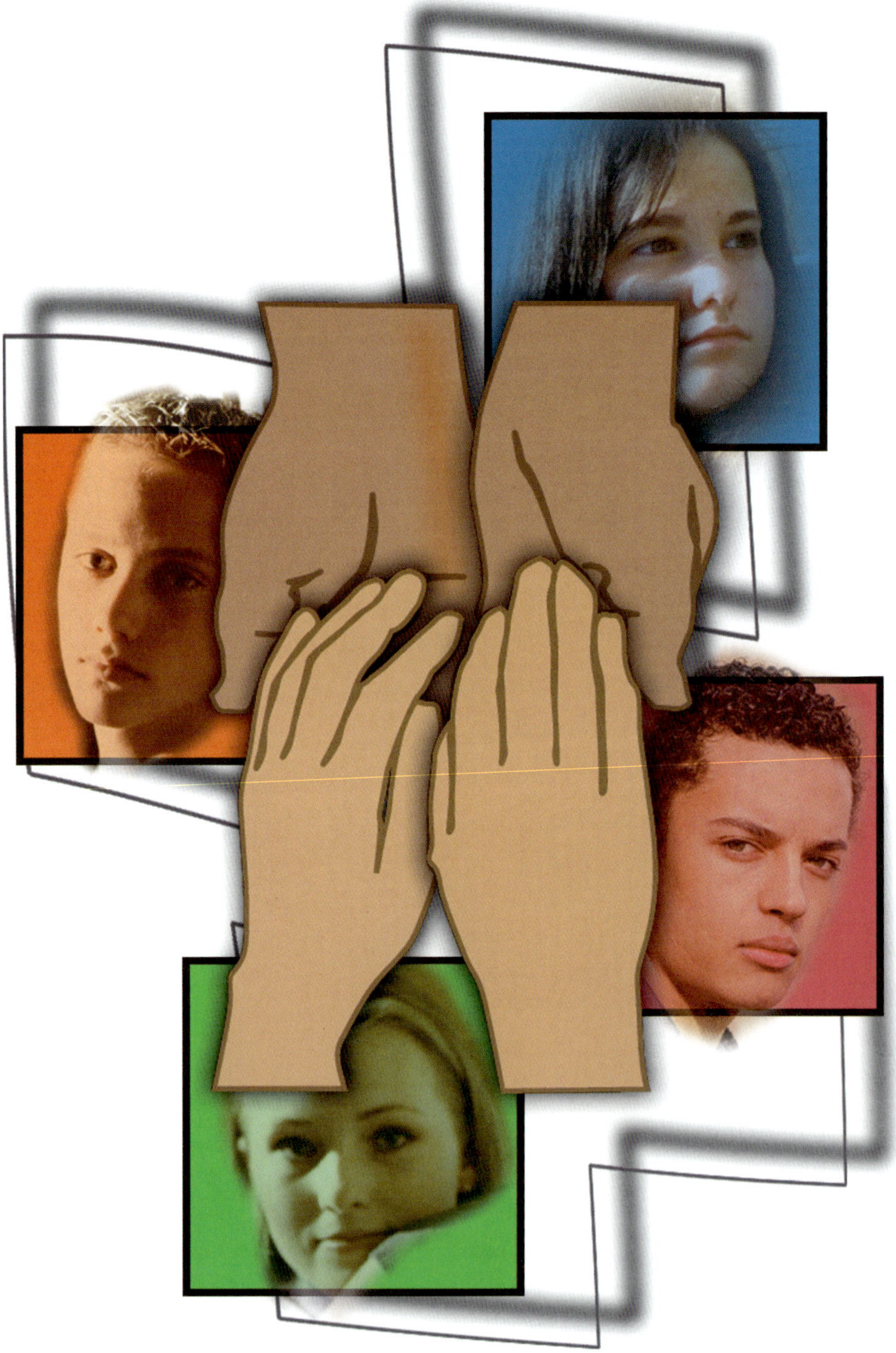

Chapter 4

Happy Birthday

Hannah felt awful. The clock on the wall, visible by the gray light creeping in through the window blinds, said it was just after 6:30. Morning had finally arrived. She'd been awake half the night throwing up. They'd said the chemo might make her a bit nauseated, but she didn't think she'd ever been so sick.

She could see her mother, sleeping in the recliner, wrapped in a hospital blanket. Throughout the night, whenever she had dozed off only to wake up vomiting again, she had felt her mother's cool hand stroking her sweat-drenched hair, her mother's arm supporting her shoulders.

Maddie and Isabel had left late last night, after the chemo drugs had finished flowing into her body. They were staying with Uncle James and Aunt Cara, although Maddie had protested that she was old enough to look after both herself and Isabel. "This is not about how capable you are," their mother had said. "It's about having your family there to support you during hard times."

Surgery had been strange. They gave Hannah anesthesia, and she started feeling drowsy; then, suddenly, it was all over. Now, she pulled up her shirt and stared at the plastic tubing sticking out from under a bandage. She sighed. She felt like a freak.

Suddenly, she realized it was her birthday. The big day she had been looking forward to for so long. She was thirteen today. So much for her party, her grown-up day of makeovers and outings. Her friends didn't even know she was in the hospital. She had last seen them at school on Thursday, but she hadn't told them about the tumor.

"What's with the crutches?" Jess had asked on Monday at lunch.

"I messed up my knee in gym class," Hannah had said, and she hadn't bothered to update the story when she'd come back to school on Wednesday.

She pictured them arriving at her empty house today for her party.

Her mother shifted her position in the recliner and opened her eyes. "How are you feeling?" she asked, her voice rough with sleep.

"Not great." She stared at the ceiling. "It's my birthday," she added after a moment.

"I know." Her mother got up and came over to sit beside Hannah. "This isn't at all what birthdays should be like. Maybe we could think of it as embarking on an adventure of survival and beating this disease."

Her mother, always the optimist. "Can't we just say it sucks?"

Her mother grimaced. "Okay. You're right. It does suck."

"Thank you."

After a breakfast Hannah didn't even want to look at, let alone eat, Mandy Wickstrom breezed into her room. "Good morning, Hannah! Time to get out of that bed and come meet some of the other children on the floor!"

"I don't really feel like getting up right now," Hannah said. Her mother had gone to Uncle James and Aunt Cara's to pick up Maddie and Isabel, and she'd been hoping to sleep until they got back.

"Well, if everyone did whatever they felt like, where would this world be? Come on now, up, up!"

Scowling, Hannah got out of bed. It seemed easier to just do what the woman wanted for now, although she fully intended to leave as soon as Mandy turned her back. Hannah put on her blue, fuzzy robe and picked up her crutches.

The room Mandy led her to had a sign beside the door that read, *The Brian Callahan Activity Room*. Under the name was a picture of a bald, smiling little boy who looked about Isabel's age. *With the help of the dedicated doctors and nurses of Pickering Memorial Hospital, Brian beat cancer. Today, he is a healthy teenager with a bright future ahead of him.*

Well, lucky for Brian, Hannah thought sarcastically. *Must be nice to have it all behind you.*

The activity room was painted a cheery yellow. Several kids played on computers along one wall, three were involved in a card game at a table in the center of the room, and a round-cheeked girl with a black bandanna tied around her head sat in an armchair near the window, reading a book. Mandy didn't even pause but headed straight for the girl with the book.

"Victoria, this is Hannah. She's new here; she had her first chemo last night. Why don't you show her around?"

The girl looked up. "Around? Around where?" She didn't look all that pleased to be interrupted.

"Show her what you kids do for fun. Tell her about our little oncology family."

The girl rolled her eyes, but put down her book. "Sure, fine, whatever."

"Good," Mandy said firmly. "I'm sure you will be wonderful friends. I need to make a few more visits, but be sure to page me if you need me."

When Mandy had gone, the girl relaxed a little. "I'm Tori," she said to Hannah. "Never ever call me Victoria. And even though I usually try to do the opposite of whatever Wicky says, I'll tell you anything you want to know about this place. I've been in and out of Pickering for fourteen months now."

Hannah wasn't sure she wanted to know much about the hospital. "What kind of cancer do you have?" she asked without thinking, and then bit her lip.

Tori frowned, and Hannah was afraid she had offended her. "Let's go back to my room." Tori stood up, tucking a bookmark into her book.

Hannah followed her uncertainly out of the activity room. When they were outside the door, Tori said, "It's a pretty strict rule that we don't talk about cancer or treatments or anything like that in the activity room; it's where we go to escape all that. Wicky shouldn't have even used the word 'oncology,' not to mention 'chemo.'"

"I'm sorry," Hannah said.

Tori shrugged. "You didn't know." They continued walking down the hall. "I have acute lymphocytic leukemia. I'm doing okay right now." She paused, then shrugged again. "This is my room."

In some ways, Tori's room looked a lot like Hannah's except that instead of the red lion poster she had a yellow hippopotamus. The hippo's head was hardly visible, however, behind the dozens of cards taped to the wall. Among the cards were several posters of black roses, dragons, and skulls. Hannah noticed one of a skeleton riding a dragon. Clothes, mostly black, were draped over the chairs, looking like any typical teenager's room.

Tori sat heavily on the bed and glanced at the chaos. "I've been here for nearly two weeks this time," she said. "The nurses don't like it, but they pretty much let me do what I like as long as my junk doesn't get in the way of their jobs. You can just push everything on the floor and sit down."

Awkwardly, Hannah balanced herself with her crutches, scooped the clothes off a chair, and dropped them on the barely visible recliner. "Do you really like it here?" she asked, sitting down.

"Like it? Of course not. What's to like about cancer? But I guess Pickering is okay."

"It's my birthday," Hannah said.

"Wow. Happy birthday. What a way to celebrate. You'd think they could have waited until Monday."

"Yeah, I don't think anybody thought about it. And I have these plastic tubes sticking out of my chest now."

"You mean a Broviac? Lots of the kids here have them. I had one for a while, but it got infected, and they had to take it out. Now I have a port-a-cath. That means they have to stick a needle into my chest every time I have chemo, but it's no big deal anymore. You'll find there are lots of fun things about cancer. Don't think I always looked this way. I used to be pretty and have hair. The cancer drugs made me gain a whole lot of weight, and of course I lost all my hair." She pulled off the bandana, revealing her bald head. Even though Hannah had been expecting it, the sight still shocked her. She reached up to touch her own thick brown hair.

"Here you are, Hannah," Mandy Wickstrom said from the doorway. "Your mother is back."

Hannah stood up. "I should go," she said to Tori. "I guess I'll see you."

"Oh, I'll probably be here," Tori said.

The first things Hannah saw when she walked into her room were the balloons. Dozens of them floated just inside the door, blocking her view of the rest of the room. Birthday balloons crowded together with cartoon characters, smiley faces, hearts, flowers, and "Get Well" balloons. Her mother must have bought out most of the store. Smiling a little, Hannah pushed through the colorful collection.

"Surprise!" The room was filled with people smiling at her. Her mother stepped forward to hug her. Looking over her mother's shoulder, Hannah saw Uncle James and Aunt Cara sitting on the chairs beside the bed. Maddie and Isabel perched on the windowsill, and Dani, Lauren, Becca, and Jess were clustered together around the recliner.

"This isn't the party we'd planned," her mother said, "but it's the best I could do on short notice."

Hannah stood there in her fuzzy bathrobe, leaning on her crutches, and stared at her mother. She wasn't sure whether to laugh or cry.

Uncle James jumped up from his chair. "Sit down, birthday girl! We brought pizza, cake, and board games. Not to mention piles of presents."

Hannah sat down on the bed slowly and looked at her family and friends; they were all smiling at her and trying to hide their worry. She loved them so much. She made herself relax a little, and decided to laugh instead of cry.

An hour later, watching Isabel collapse on the bed in helpless giggles over a game of mad libs, Hannah could almost forget where she was and what was happening to her body. She hadn't eaten any pizza and only a few bites of the cake—the memory of last night's nausea was still too strong—but for a while her fears about the future were drowned out and she was happier than she had been in days.

Types of Cancer in Teens

Though the rate of cancer in teens is increasing, it is important to keep in mind that it is still rare in kids between thirteen and seventeen. Still, there are some forms of cancer that are more likely to be diagnosed in teens than in adults.

Leukemia

Among children of all ages, leukemia is the most common cancer. Leukemia is a blood disorder. White blood cells are created in such large numbers that they fill the bone marrow, making it difficult for the body to produce the other types of blood cells it needs to be healthy, like red blood cells and platelets. These white blood cells are defective, so they cannot perform their normal function, helping the body to fight off infection and disease. Because of the lack of healthy blood cells, the person with leukemia becomes anemic, suffers from excessive bleeding, and has an increased risk of infection.

The two leukemias most likely to be diagnosed in teens are acute lymphocytic leukemia (ALL) and acute myelogenous leukemia (AML). ALL is the most common of all cancers in teens. Treatment for ALL and AML usually begins with chemotherapy, and some receive external radiation therapy. A relatively new treatment method—stem-cell transplants—has had promising results. In this method, the person with leukemia receives new stem cells from a cancer-free person. Bone marrow transplants are a common form of stem-cell transfer.

The cure rate for some forms of leukemia is quite good when the cancer is diagnosed and treatment begins early. Most people who have recovered from ALL and AML never have a recurrence.

Osteosarcoma

Osteosarcoma is the most common of the bone cancers, is seen more often in males than females, and is more prevalent in taller people. Individuals with certain genetically caused disorders (such as the eye tumor retinoblastoma) or who have received radiation therapy for other types of cancer appear to be more prone to osteosarcoma.

Because osteosarcoma tends to be diagnosed during the growth spurt years, the initial pain and discomfort are sometimes attributed to the normal growth process—growing pains. Eventually, the pain becomes excessive, and swelling and lumps occur in an arm or leg. For many, the pain and swelling are worse at night or during exercise. Generally, the cancer is found near the knee. Osteosarcoma tumors seldom, but can, metastasize to other parts of the arm or leg.

Treatment for osteosarcoma usually begins with a course of chemotherapy and is followed with surgery to remove the tumor. More chemotherapy or radiation therapy may follow. As a last resort, it might be necessary to amputate the affected limb. In the past, amputation meant the removal of the entire limb. Today, however, most surgeons try to perform limb-***salvage*** surgery. This type of surgery removes only the bone with the cancer, leaving the rest of the limb. A bone **graft** or metal rod fills the gap left by the bone removal.

Almost all teens receiving chemotherapy for osteosarcoma face side effects, including hair loss, nausea, bleeding, infections, and skin problems. Those for whom amputation is necessary must also deal with the complete or partial loss of an entire arm or leg. For them, counseling, physical therapy, and the advances of modern-day **prostheses** can help them live an active life. Fortunately, most teens win their battle with osteosarcoma.

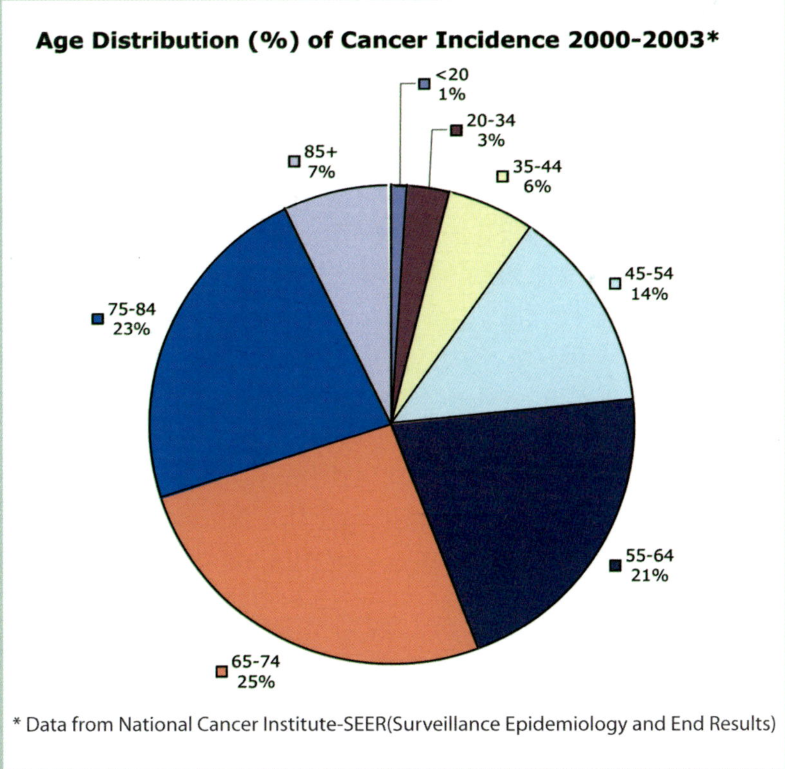

As shown in this chart, cancer is still rare in people under 20 years of age. However, rates have been increasing, and there are certain types of cancer that are more likely to be diagnosed in teens than adults.

Ewing's Sarcoma

Ewing's sarcoma is another bone cancer that most often occurs in teens. The disease is almost always found in the leg or pelvis. The treatment choice is generally surgery and chemotherapy. In some cases, radiation is used instead of or as an ***adjunct*** to surgery.

Potential side effects for those in treatment for Ewing's sarcoma are the same as those with osteosarcoma. Most teens survive this form of cancer as well.

Lymphoma

The human body uses the lymphatic system to fight infection. The lymph nodes, thymus, spleen, tonsils, and bone marrow all work together to battle these foreign invaders. Lymphoma refers to cancer that occurs within that lymphatic system, making the body unable to fight germs and infections, leaving the body prone to many illnesses. Most teens with lymphoma have either Hodgkin's disease or non-Hodgkin's lymphoma.

Hodgkin's disease is most often diagnosed in teens and young adults. It is cancer of the lymph nodes and is often found in the neck, armpits, chest, or thighs, although it can appear wherever lymph nodes are found. The primary symptom of the disease is swelling or a lump in one or more of the areas listed above; it is not painful. Diagnosis is made by a microscopic examination of the tissue removed through a biopsy. Treatment protocol calls for chemotherapy and sometimes radiation.

Non-Hodgkin's lymphoma has many of the characteristics of ALL. On examination, white blood cells are found in the lymph nodes. Symptoms are often the same for both ALL and non-Hodgkin's lymphoma. Chemotherapy is usually the treatment choice for non-Hodgkin's lymphoma.

For those who have completed their treatment, a complete remission and no recurrence can be expected.

Barry Watson

He was young, handsome, and a star of the hit television show *7th Heaven*. Barry Watson had found success in Hollywood. Then, in 2002, his life changed

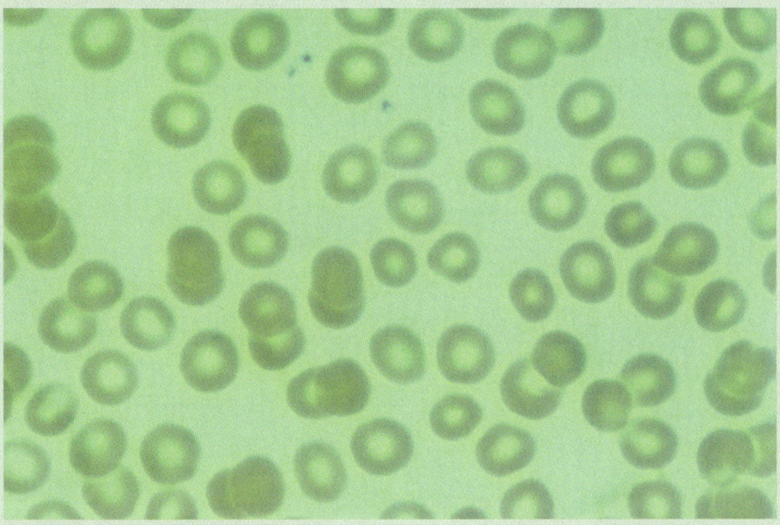

Leukemia is the most common cancer among children. It is a blood disorder, which causes the body to produce defective white blood cells, which multiply out of control and crowd out other blood cells.

when he was diagnosed with Hodgkin's disease. Barry took some time off from acting to concentrate on getting well. When Barry's cancer went into remission, he returned to acting. Though not appearing in every episode of *7th Heaven*, his character, Matt Camden, makes frequent appearances. Barry is also working on a growing film career.

Lance Armstrong

His name is synonymous with courage and success—and cancer.

No name is better known in the world of bicycle racing than Lance Armstrong. He began his athletic career as a **triathlete**, but by age seventeen had decided to concentrate on bicycle racing. It didn't take long before he began to dominate the sport. His dominance of the **arduous** Tour de France was unprecedented and, to some, unbelievable. Lance has often been the subject of accusations that he took performance-enhancing drugs to help him win seven consecutive Tour de France competitions. After all, no one before had ever been so successful. None of the allegations were proven, and for most fans, Lance's image remains untarnished. In 1996, few would have thought that Lance would reach such heights.

On October 2, 1996, the Texas native was diagnosed with testicular cancer—the most common cancer in males between the ages of fifteen and thirty-five. But, the cancer was not confined to a testicle; it had already spread to Lance's lungs and brain. His doctors told him that his chances of beating the cancer were 40 percent. (After Lance had recovered, one of his doctors told him that the 40 percent figure was only meant to give him hope; his actual chance of survival was as little as 3 percent.) Surgeons removed a testicle and two brain **lesions**, and Lance was advised to follow surgery with chemotherapy. Lance had two types of chemotherapy from which to choose, and he decided to undergo the more aggressive form of chemotherapy. The more traditional form would have left him with reduced lung capacity, bringing his cycling career to an end; while the aggressive chemotherapy would be more difficult to handle, it would leave his lung capacity intact. His treatment was successful, and as soon as his cancer went into remission, Lance returned to training. In 1998, he was again racing professionally.

A cancer diagnosis does not mean the end of your life. Lance Armstrong had his most successful years after his diagnosis, winning his battle with testicular cancer and then racing to victory in the Tour de France seven straight times.

After he won his battle with cancer, Lance established the Lance Armstrong Foundation. The LiveStrong program supports people with cancer and survivors and provides educational programs to increase cancer awareness. Their biggest fundraiser is the yellow LiveStrong wristband, which sells for US$1.00. As of January 2006, more than 58 million wristbands have been sold worldwide. Athletic-wear company Nike is also planning a line of shoes carrying the "Live Strong" yellow in support of the foundation and its projects.

Lance has retired from professional bicycling, but not from his work on behalf of cancer awareness. He is a frequent visitor to hospitals to visit people with cancer and is a popular and effective speaker on the subject. He **epitomizes** the fact that cancer can be beaten.

Cancer-Fighting Goes Video

When he was nine years old, the Make-a-Wish Foundation asked Ben Duskin, who was undergoing treatment for leukemia, what wish he would like fulfilled. Most of the time the organization gets requests for trips or to meet celebrities. But, Ben's wish was different. Like most children his age, Ben loved video games. He wanted a video game to help people with cancer take their minds off of painful chemotherapy, at least for a little while.

LucasFilms agreed to donate their high-tech facilities during nonoperation hours, and LucasArts software engineer Eric Johnston donated his time to work with Ben on the game. The main character

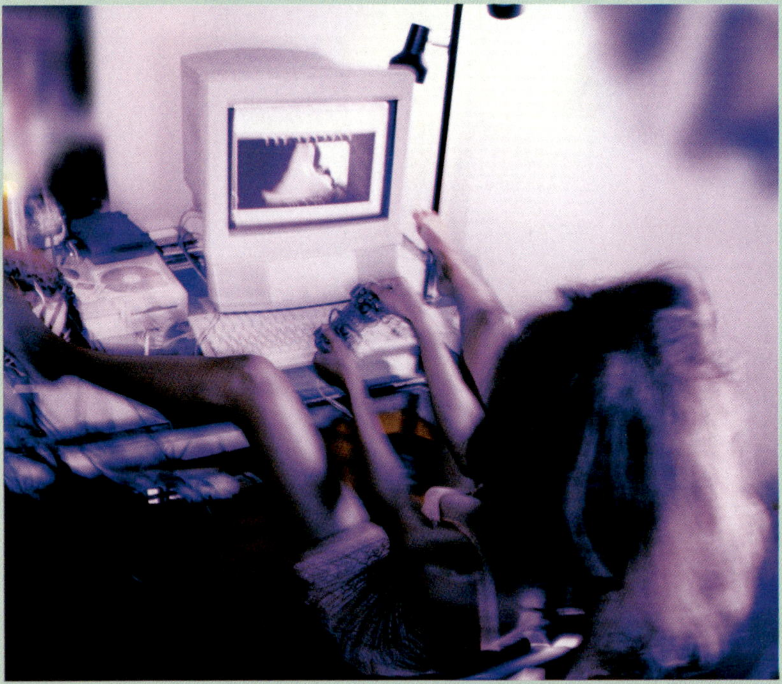

Video games are a popular pastime for children and adolescents. Ben's Game, available for free from Make-a-Wish, was created at the request of a child with cancer as an activity to help people with cancer get their minds off treatment for a little while.

(who is based on Ben) races around on a skateboard, blasting cancer cells and collecting shields to protect against the most common chemotherapy side effects. In 2004, Ben's Game was launched on the Make-a-Wish Foundation's Web site. It is available in nine languages and can be downloaded for free (www.makewish.org/ben).

Ben's leukemia is in remission. In November 2005, Ben and Eric Johnston were honored by the Dalai Lama as Unsung Heroes of Compassion.

Chapter 5

The Complications of Cancer

"It's not that they don't like you anymore," Becca said. "I think they just don't know how to handle the cancer. They don't like how it makes them think about their own mortality." Only Becca would use a word like mortality in normal conversation.

"I miss them," Hannah said. "Weren't they okay at my birthday party?" They were sitting on her bed at home talking. Becca had been coming over a lot when Hannah was out of the hospital. Jess would still talk to her a little when she went to school—which wasn't all that often anymore—but Dani and Lauren practically ignored her.

"Well, we'd all just found out you had cancer that day. It hadn't really sunk in yet. Now you're missing a lot of school, and you're starting to look a little different, and they just want to pretend it isn't happening."

"I'd like to pretend it isn't happening, too—but then some nurse always comes along and tries to stick a needle in me. What do you mean, I look different? I haven't lost my hair."

"You've lost weight and you have big dark circles under your eyes. Sometimes you look fine, but sometimes you look really sick."

"I've been really tired." Hannah was halfway through her second cycle of chemo, and the exhaustion was almost worse than the vomiting. The chemo drugs made her horribly sick for a few days, but she was tired all the time.

"No kidding," Becca said. "I'd say you had an excuse."

"Girls!" Hannah's mother called from downstairs. "It's about time for supper."

Hannah pulled her crutches over and stood up. As she stood, a wave of dizziness hit her. Suddenly, her skin felt icy and clammy, and sparkles danced in front of her eyes.

"Are you okay?" Becca asked. "You just went completely white."

Hannah closed her eyes. "Just a minute." She stood very still until the dizziness passed and her head stopped spinning. "I think I'll be all right now." She opened her eyes. She felt better, although now she had a headache.

Becca was looking at her with concern. "Are you sure you're okay?"

"Yeah, I think I stood up too fast."

By bedtime that night, Hannah's headache had gotten worse instead of better. To make matters worse, her throat was starting to feel sore and scratchy. She got ready for bed slowly, crawled under the covers, and fell asleep.

She woke up in the middle of the night, shaking with cold. Her blankets didn't seem to be warming her up at all. She found her crutches and struggled down the hall to her mother's room, feeling strange and disoriented.

"Mom, wake up," she whispered, shaking her mother's shoulder.

Her mother rolled over. "Hannah? What's wrong?"

"Do we have any more blankets? I'm really cold."

She felt her mother's hand on her cheek. "You're burning up!" Her mother turned on the bedside light and sat up. "Sit down. I'm going to go get the thermometer."

When her mother came back with the thermometer, Hannah was lying down with the blankets pulled tight around her.

"104.2," her mother said when the thermometer beeped. "I'm going to call the hospital."

"Can I have another blanket first?"

The rest of the night was a blur. Hannah dozed in her mother's bed, piled high with blankets but still shivering. She heard people's voices now and then, buzzing at the edges of her consciousness. Eventually, she felt herself being lifted. She opened her eyes for a moment and saw Uncle James' face above her. She closed her eyes again.

She woke up out of a tangle of dark dreams, feeling weak and wrung out. Her head still ached and her throat hurt, but her mind felt clearer and she wasn't as cold. She was back at Pickering, lying in a hospital bed. This room had a green rhinoceros on the wall.

"You're awake!" Hannah turned her head to see her mother sitting in one of the hospital's straight-backed chairs.

"What happened?"

"You had an infection. They gave you antibiotics when we brought you in last night, and your fever broke this morning."

"When can I go home?" Hannah had gotten used to being in the hospital, but she would still rather be at home, in her own room, in a place where they didn't wake her up in the middle of the night to check her vitals.

"I don't know," her mother said, "but probably not today."

Later in the day, Hannah still felt weak, but she was better enough to start getting bored. She decided to go down to the activity room to see who was there. She usually spent a lot of time hanging out with Tori, if she was in Pickering at the same time as Hannah, but she had also met other kids her age—Lucy and Andrew who had leukemia like Tori, and Henry who had a brain tumor.

Hannah wrapped her robe around her shoulders and began to brush her hair. It was tangled, and the brush caught. She tugged, but instead of loosening the tangle, the entire clump of hair came out. Her heart pounding, she stared with horror at the hair in the brush. Then she ran her fingers through her hair; more clumps came out, handfuls of it. Dr. Stratton had told her this would probably happen, although chemo didn't make everyone lose their hair, but she still wasn't prepared.

She had always had hair like her mother's—thick, messy curls that barely looked brushed even at the best of times. Her hair had sometimes frustrated and annoyed her, but that didn't mean she wanted to be bald. She looked at the hair in her lap, and her eyes filled with tears.

Her blurred gaze traveled desperately around the room, looking for she didn't know what, but her gaze caught on a container of nursing supplies. She dumped the hair in the wastebasket beside the bed and struggled to her feet with her crutches. In the container, she found a pair of scissors, used for cutting bandages.

She limped into the bathroom and looked at herself in the mirror. Her hair hung past her shoulders, but she could already see patches of her scalp where it had fallen out. She closed her eyes for a moment and took a deep breath. Then she attacked her hair with the scissors, cutting as close to her head as she could. She refused to look at the mirror as she cut.

When she could run her hand over her head and not find anything long enough to pull, she finally stopped. Hair was everywhere—the counter, the sink, the floor. Her head felt lighter. At last, she looked in the mirror again and caught her breath. Her remaining hair was uneven, scraggly, and very, very short. Her face was different; her head looked bigger and her eyes were now in the middle of her face instead of at the top. She didn't like it at all, and yet she felt strangely triumphant. *She* had done this, not the cancer or the chemo. It didn't matter that it would have all fallen out anyway; she had chosen when and how. On this bad day, the fact that she taken control of her life, if only in a small way, made her just a little bit happier.

Treating Cancer

For many years, the diagnosis of cancer seemed to be an automatic death sentence. In some cases, medical personnel provided only **palliative care**, and the patient and family waited for death to occur. Fortunately, this has changed. As research led to a better understanding of cancer and its causes and treatments, life expectancy increased for those with cancer. Today, though not all cancers are curable, most are treatable, especially the ones children, adolescents, and young adults are most likely to develop.

Surgery

One of the most common forms of treating cancer is surgery. Depending on the cancer's location, the operation can sometimes be performed in a doctor's office or as a hospital outpatient. The cancerous tissue is removed, and the surgeon often removes some of the tissue (lymph nodes, for example) surrounding it. A pathologist will check the surrounding tissue to see if the cancer has spread beyond its original location. In some cases, surgery will be the only treatment required. In others, the oncologist will recommend that surgery be followed by a period of chemotherapy or radiation, or a combination of both.

Chemotherapy

The use of drugs to treat cancer is called chemotherapy. Not all cancers respond to this treatment, but it is very effective for many forms of the disease. Sometimes the therapy consists of one drug, though the preferred treatment in other cases may be a "drug cocktail" consisting of two or more medications. Although the first chemotherapy may be given while the individual is hospitalized, it is most often provided on an outpatient basis. The individual generally sits in a chair while the drugs are given **intravenously**. The frequency of treatment varies with the medications, type of cancer, and health of the individual. The drugs kill the cancerous cells, but sometimes harm healthy ones as well, though most healthy cells recover when chemotherapy is over. Many researchers believe that the loss of the healthy cells may be the reason for some of the side effects of chemotherapy.

Some individuals taking chemotherapy have many side effects, some have few, and a very small number of individuals have no side effects at all. In general, the types and severity of side effects depend on the types of drugs being used. Individuals undergoing "chemo" may report having a metallic taste in their mouths while receiving the drugs. More common side effects may include

- hair loss
- nausea
- fatigue
- loss of appetite
- diarrhea
- mouth and lip sores

Doctors can provide medications to help the individual deal with most of the side effects, and many individuals use scarves, hats, or even wigs to hide hair loss. It is important to remember that not everyone who has chemo will encounter these side effects. The hair will grow back, and in most cases, the other side effects go away when chemotherapy is completed.

Radiation

Radiation has proven to be an effective treatment for some forms of cancer. There are primarily two forms of radiation treatments for cancer, external or internal radiation. In externally provided radiation therapy, high-frequency waves are aimed at the affected area from a machine, and treatment is usually received on an outpatient basis. Radioactive materials contained in needles or seeds are implanted in or near the tumor in internal radiation therapy. The implants can be temporary or permanent.

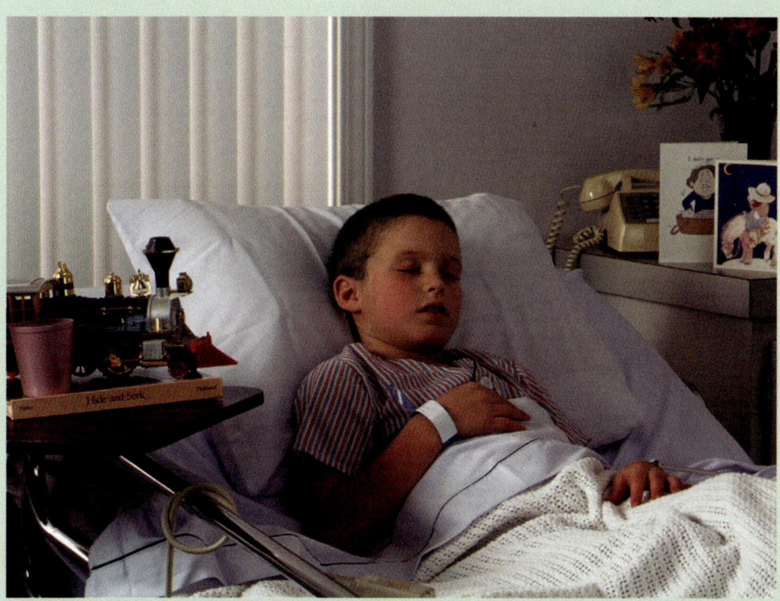

Chemotherapy and radiation are usually a patient's best chance for remission. Unfortunately, both affect healthy cells as well as cancerous ones, resulting in unpleasant side effects like hair loss and nausea.

Potential side effects from radiation therapy are generally temporary and include fatigue, hair loss, and skin irritation. There is an additional side effect with internal radiation therapy. During the initial stages of treatment, patients on this form of therapy are often required to stay in the hospital, away from the other patients, while radioactivity levels are high. The patient will have to stay in the hospital until the levels in permanent implants have dropped to a safe level. No radioactivity remains in the body once the temporary implants are removed.

Hormone Therapy

Some cancers, such as breast cancer, depend on **hormones** for growth. Doctors often use hormone

A patient receiving internal radiation has radioactive materials implanted in or near the tumor. Because of the high levels of radiation, patients may have to stay in a separate area of the hospital.

therapy to treat these forms of cancer. Drugs are used to either stop the production of certain hormones or to change the way they work. Another form of hormone therapy is to remove the organ that produces the hormone; in breast cancer, this means the ovaries would be removed.

Hormone therapy can have many side effects, including

- fatigue
- fluid retention
- weight gain
- hot flashes
- nausea and vomiting
- changes in appetite
- blood clots
- bone loss in ***premenopausal*** women

Unlike side effects of most other treatment methods, the ones associated with hormone therapy may be permanent.

Biological Therapy

A newer cancer treatment method uses the body's own immune system to fight disease. Interferon, interleukin-2, and colony-stimulating factors are examples of biological therapy.

This treatment method is not without side effects, but they depend on the specific therapy being used. Among the possible side effects are flu-like symptoms and the tendency to bleed or bruise easily. Like most of the other treatment methods, side effects generally disappear when treatment is completed.

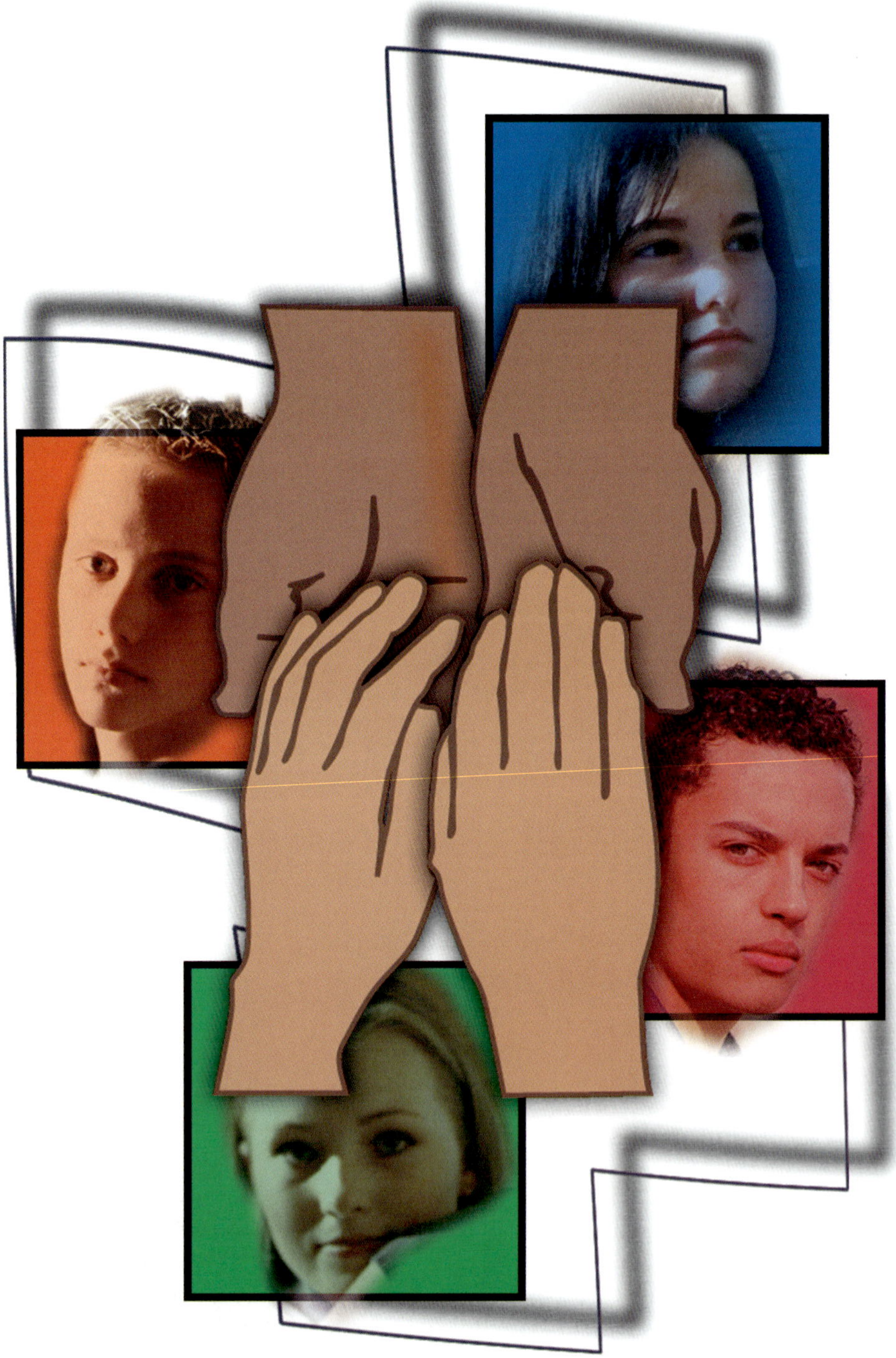

Chapter 6

Losing the Tumor

The activity room was filled with music and laughter. A group of clowns juggled brightly colored balls, pretended to fight, and made faces at the little kids. Hannah sat in a back corner with Tori, Henry, and Lucy, feeling cranky. She had had a chemo treatment two days before and was still feeling some low-level nausea whenever she moved. She also had so many mouth sores that she couldn't have eaten if she wanted to. Her mother and sisters were at Isabel's dance recital. Hannah was just as glad she was in the hospital for it, because she wouldn't have wanted to go anyway and her mother would have made her.

Tori was in a dark mood, too. She wore black flannel pants, a black long-sleeved T-shirt with a picture of a vampire bat on it, and her usual black bandanna, but she had added black eyeliner and black lipstick today as well. She glowered at the clowns. "It's depressing to think that they only came to distract us from the fact that we're all dying."

"We're sick, not dying," Henry said patiently. This argument had been going on a while.

"The kids are so cute." Lucy was the only one of the four of them who currently had any hair, although hers was not much more than an inch long. She was wearing khaki and looked like a frail army cadet. Her current chemo was an experimental drug that did not cause hair loss and was somehow supposed to be both more effective and gentler.

A pretty, young black woman who had been talking to a little girl and her mother walked over to Hannah and her friends and sat down with them. She dropped her brightly colored knit bag to the floor beside her. "Hi," she said. "I'm Rachel. Are you enjoying the party?"

"Sure," Henry said.

Hannah and Tori didn't say anything.

After a small pause, Lucy said, "The party's fine for the kids, but we're just a little old for it, you see."

Rachel laughed. "I didn't think anyone was too old for clowns," she said. "Now, tell me your names."

"Are you a new nurse?" Tori asked, after they had introduced themselves.

"I'm new, but I'm not exactly a nurse," Rachel said. "My job is to help you deal with the all the emotional stuff that comes with fighting cancer and being in the hospital."

"Did you replace Mrs. Zithlow?" Henry asked. Mrs. Zithlow was a counselor who had worked at Pickering, until her own health problems had forced her to retire. Hannah had only met her once, during her first hospital stay.

"Yes, I did," Rachel answered. "Here," she said, opening her bag, "I brought you all a present." She pulled out four books and gave one to each of them. They were small, with dark green cloth covers.

"It's blank," Hannah said, opening hers.

"It's a journal," Rachel said. "It can be helpful to write down what you're thinking or feeling."

"I have a journal already," said Tori.

"Well, you can use this one when that one gets full," Rachel said.

"If I live that long," Tori muttered under her breath.

Rachel stood up; Hannah wasn't sure if she had heard Tori's remark. "I'll leave you to keep not enjoying the party, but I'll be seeing you all again. And if there is anything you want to talk about before then, come find me."

"She probably thinks you're the problem patient now," Hannah said to Tori when Rachel had gone.

"I *am* the problem patient," Tori retorted.

"You just want everyone to think that," Lucy said calmly. "Really you're just a sweetie pie."

Henry snorted and they all laughed.

They were still laughing a moment later when Dr. Stratton walked over to them.

"I'm glad to see you're having a good time," the oncologist said. "Hannah, I'd like to talk to you for a minute."

Immediately, they stopped laughing, and Hannah felt fear tighten her stomach. He looked at their faces. "Oh, goodness no," he said. "It's nothing terrible. Do you think I'd pull you out of a party to give you bad news?"

"You might if it was bad enough," Tori said, as Hannah eased herself to her feet and got her crutches.

"Really, it's good news," Dr. Stratton said to Hannah when they got out into the hall. "I'm sorry for interrupting the party, but I'm leaving for a conference in a few minutes, and I wanted to talk to you before I left. I've already called your mother and talked to her."

They walked back to Hannah's room, and she sat down on the bed.

"The results of the scan we did last night show that the tumor has shrunk even more than we'd hoped." Dr. Stratton sat in a chair and leaned his elbows on his knees. "So what we're going to do is stop the chemotherapy right now. You can go home tomorrow and relax for a couple of weeks.

Then, you can come back and we'll do the surgery to remove the tumor."

Hannah caught her breath. "Does this mean that I'm almost done?"

"It means that, yes, if all goes well, you're getting closer to being done. It's going to take some time for your leg to heal after the surgery. What we'll be doing is taking out the tumor and a bit of the healthy bone and tissue around it—just to be sure we get everything. Because of the location of the tumor, we will remove your entire knee and then replace it with an artificial joint."

"You're going to take out my knee?" Hannah was startled. "Will I be able to walk?"

"Absolutely," Dr. Stratton said. "You'll have physical therapy, and that will help you work on strengthening your leg muscles and adjusting to the implant. Artificial joints are getting better all the time, but you still might need follow-up surgeries sometime in the future, to clean or adjust the implant. There's also a chance of infection. You need to know that, but I want to tell you that even twenty years ago, osteosarcoma like you have would almost always have meant an amputation. Today, it's a whole new ballgame."

After Dr. Stratton left, Hannah didn't know whether to feel happy or terrified. Of course, she had known she would have surgery before long, but the idea that in two weeks she would have a fake knee was unsettling. She looked at the journal Rachel had given her, but her emotions were too complicated to write down; besides, she wasn't sure she even wanted to figure them out. Of course it was good that they were going to take out the tumor, but they were taking out her *knee*, too.

February 4

Okay, so maybe I'll try writing in here. Tomorrow they are going to knock me out and cut out my knee. I still don't want to think about that much. It makes me want to throw up. Mrs. Ellis, my history teacher, gave me a book about a guy named Terry Fox who had osteosarcoma in his leg. They cut off his leg, since they didn't do much with fake knees back in the 1970s. Then, because he was such a great guy, he tried to run across Canada on his artificial leg to raise money for cancer research. But his cancer came back before he made it and he died. I suppose this is supposed to be an inspirational story and proves that I'll still be able to run after they cut me up. But he died. *I don't know how that's supposed to make me feel better.*

Mom wants me to talk to her—and I do—but a couple of weeks ago I found her crying in the bathroom. She said she was really okay, but I don't think I believe her. I don't want to upset her. I don't want to tell her that I'm so scared, that I'm afraid I'm going to open my eyes after the surgery and look down and see only one leg, that the doctor will say, "I'm sorry but the cancer has spread." That I will die.

Hannah lay on her back on a narrow metal operating table. People wearing medical scrubs and masks moved between her and the bright, round ceiling light.

"We're going to take good care of you, Hannah," Dr. Stratton said into her ear. "Dr. Li will be doing your surgery; she's one of the best."

A woman bent over her. "Okay, Hannah, I want you to start at one hundred and count backward for me."

"One hundred," Hannah whispered shakily, looking at the light. "Ninety-nine. Ninety-eight. Ninety-seven. . ."

The light seemed to twist and she blinked. The light was gone. She was in a different room, a curtain pulled around the bed. Her throat hurt and her mouth was dry. Her body felt heavy, and her brain was fuzzy. She could hear voices on the other side of the curtain.

After a moment, she realized she was in the recovery room and that the surgery was over. Then she remembered her leg. She struggled to push herself up from the bed and finally was able to roll her head around to look down at her lower body. Under the sheet, she could see that both her legs went all the way down to her feet, with a bigger bump at her left knee than her right. She still had both legs. She closed her eyes again and let herself relax.

The Texas Children's Cancer Center and Hematology Service has these tips for teens living with cancer:

- Exercise.

  walk

  hike

  swim

But avoid contact sports if your platelet count is low. And be sure to use sunscreen anytime you're outside.

- Watch your weight.

To gain weight:

  drink milkshakes

  dip veggies in peanut butter

  add cheese to any food

To lose weight:

  eat fat-free or low-fat foods

  eat lean meats

  stay away from fried foods

- Take care of your appearance.

If you are receiving chemotherapy, be sure to talk with a doctor or nurse before you:

  get a tattoo

  have any part of your body pierced (including ears)

  shave anything, even if you've shaved it in the past

Coping with the Visible Side Effects

Although most side effects of cancer treatment are temporary, it can be difficult to deal with the visible ones when they occur. Sometimes it's just not enough to say things like "It'll go away when this is over" or "It'll be worth it in the end." Especially when that person's a teenager.

Teen years are all about change. Children's interests mature into those of teenagers, and an interest that takes on increasing importance is appearance.

As with part of any life, diet and exercise should play an important role in living with cancer. Be sure to check with your doctor or nurse about what is best for you.

Whether or not there is too much emphasis placed on appearance, the fact is that teens—male and female—care about how they look. And if a teen looks "different"—no matter how good the reason—it can make a difficult situation almost unbearable.

That's where programs such as Look Good . . . Feel Better for Teens come in. This is a free program for boys and girls between the ages of thirteen and seventeen who are going through cancer treatment, in most cases chemotherapy.

Look Good . . . Feel Better for Teens is offered online (www.2bMe.com) or at hospitals in several U.S. cities. Teens are given advice about makeup, skin care, school, head coverings, and many other topics. But, they get more than advice. They learn they are not alone.

Many hospitals offer support groups for teens undergoing cancer treatment. Members of such a group at Memorial Sloan-Kettering Hospital in New York City came up with this advice to those they deal with in and out of the hospital:

- Please ask me how I'm feeling—not my parents. I know.
- When I'm in the hospital, ask me personal questions in private.
- Parents should relax more because everything is going to be OK.
- Please pay attention to my feelings when I need help. Be there for me and I'll understand.

A teen with cancer may feel like she cannot talk about how she is feeling. A support group made up of other teens with cancer may help her open up and realize she is not alone.

- Knock before you enter my room, whether it's at the hospital or at home.
- Let me be me!

Learning to Cope

The diagnosis of cancer is never easy to deal with. Some individuals might have to spend time—sometimes a long time—in the hospital, but eventually, most will be able to go home and get on with life, though treatment schedules, medications, and tests become a large part of that life for a while. Everyone connected with the individual undergoing treatment will have to

Going back to school can be difficult for an adolescent with cancer as well as for his friends and teachers. Honesty about the situation will help both sides cope with the adjustment.

learn to adjust to a new definition of normal; things can't be as they were before.

At first, some might feel as though they only want to stay in their rooms, hidden away from the outside world. But, that safety net may not be what's best for the person in the long term. Most experts agree that it is important to return to previous activities as much as possible and as soon as possible.

A big part of kids' lives is school, and returning to school after discovering one has cancer can be terrifying—for both the person with cancer and her friends. At first, neither may know what to say. It's not as though someone has just been away on vacation after all. Most of the teen's friends have probably not had a peer diagnosed with cancer before. Everyone will probably feel strange and awkward, even afraid, in the beginning. On the Web site Teens Living with Cancer, Tory wrote about the fear in returning to school:

I was terrified and constantly wondering if people were going to laugh or even reject me for the way I looked. Before I left for school my father gave me a bit of advice that has stuck with me since. He said, "Throughout your life, you will come to realize that you'll be able to count your true friends with one hand. So, today at school, you'll see who's who."

He was right. People who I had thought were my friends looked at me as if I were a creature from Mars. When all was said and done, however, the few people who spoke to me were and still are my true friends. Every one of them told me it doesn't matter what's on the outside; it's what's on the inside that counts.

Okay, it's pretty realistic to think that some people might not want to have anything to do with the returning student, but how does one deal with the others, and with the curiosity that is only natural?

Honestly. The teen may have been the subject of many rumors during her absence. One teen reported that a rumor had circulated her school that her three-month absence was because she was pregnant! If

Experts agree that getting back into a previous routine is important for an individual with cancer. More than anything else, caring support from teachers, friends, and family will help a child with cancer readjust to a "normal" schedule.

people know the truth, there's no place for rumors. Be honest about what is going on. But it is not necessary to always give out complete details. Everyone—even teens—needs privacy, and if one isn't comfortable telling someone every little detail of an illness or treatment, he should not feel obligated to do so.

Sometimes returning students will need some physical help from friends. Most friends are willing to help, but often don't because they don't want the person to feel as though he is being pitied. And, most teens with cancer don't want anyone's pity. When asked what the difference between caring about someone and pitying someone, one teen described it this way: "Caring is treating you as you, not as someone with cancer. That's pity." Again, dealing with each other honestly is the best way to avoid this conflict.

Fellow students are not the only ones who may feel awkward when a teen with cancer returns to school. For many teachers, this may be the first time they have had a student with cancer. Some experts recommend that the student, parents, and medical professional meet with the teacher to let him know what to expect with the student's return, including any physical changes and assistance that might be required. This not only helps the teacher work with the situation, but also gives the teacher information that could prove beneficial in helping the student adjust to the class and the class to the student.

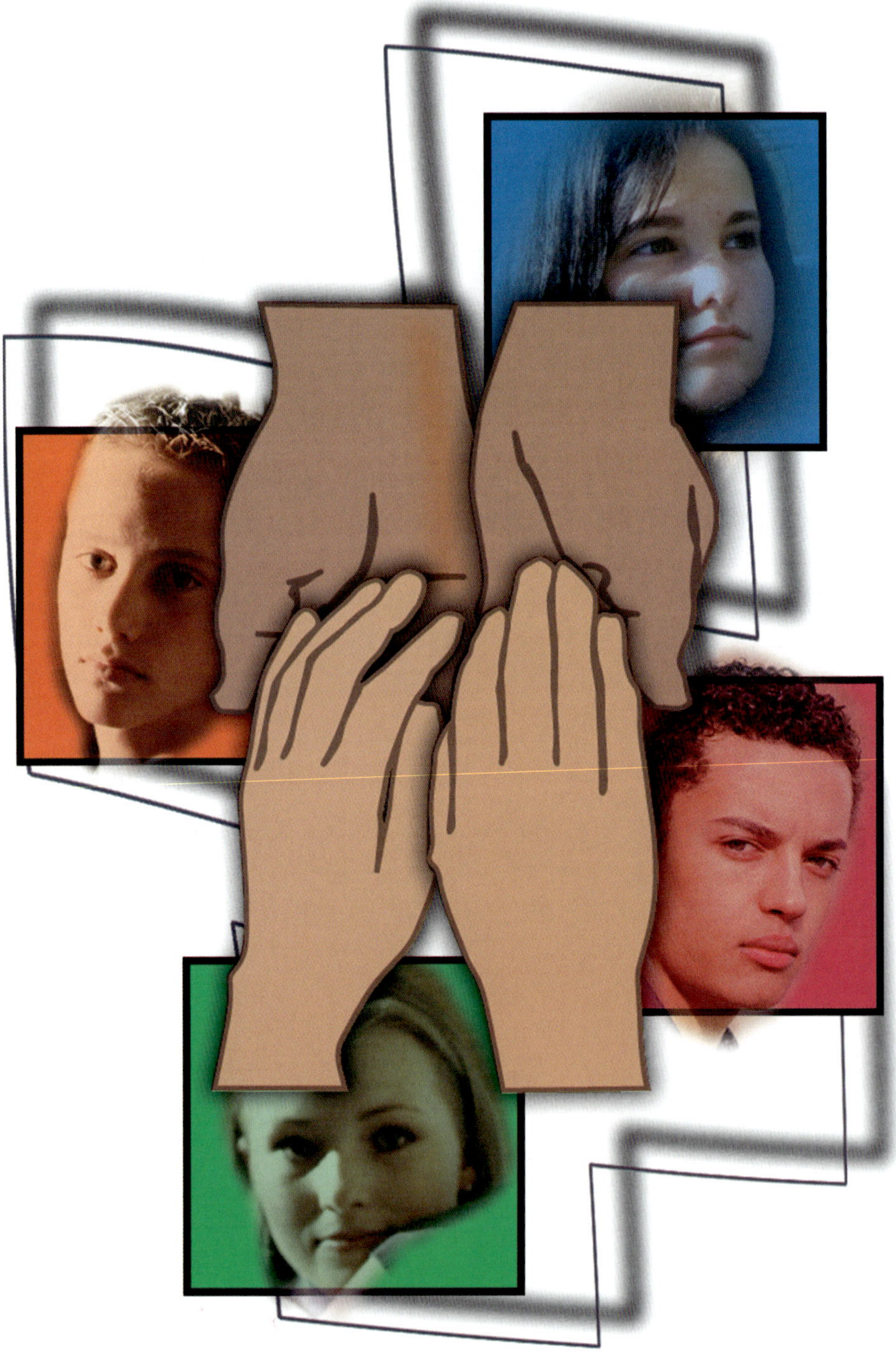

Chapter 7

Only the Good

Hannah closed her eyes and tried to doze. A plastic bag connected to the Broviac in her chest fed a cocktail of cisplatin and doxorubin into her body. Her leg ached, and exhaustion flowed through her with the chemotherapy drugs.

Amy, her physical therapist, had pushed her hard that morning, forcing her to put weight on her leg. Hannah was back to using two crutches, like she had been before the surgery. For a long time, though, she had had to use a wheelchair while her leg healed. In some ways, she preferred the wheelchair. When Amy made her try to stand on her own, Hannah was sometimes gripped by a fear that her leg would splinter and break, the artificial knee twisting into a useless wreck.

She must have fallen asleep, but her mother's hand stroking her head through the purple fleece hat Maddie had made for her dragged Hannah back to consciousness. As soon as Hannah opened her eyes, she knew something was wrong. Her mother's eyes were just a little too sparkly and wet, her lips pressed together a little too tightly.

"What happened?" she whispered. Her mouth was dry and sore, and her throat was scratchy.

Her mother sighed and squeezed her eyes shut without answering. Tears seeped out from under her eyelids and ran down her face.

"What happened?" Hannah repeated. Fear, like sickness, curled in her stomach. "Was it the scan? Did the cancer come back?"

"It's Lucy," her mother said. "She died this morning."

Instantly, an overwhelming jumble of emotions flooded through her: relief that it wasn't the scans that had made her mother cry, shame both for thinking of her own cancer first and for her relief, and indescribable bewilderment at the idea of Lucy dead. She knew of two other patients who had died while she was being treated at Pickering, but she hadn't known them personally. They were both a lot younger than she was, and a lot sicker than Lucy had seemed.

"No," she said. "Lucy was my friend."

"I know."

"But Lucy was at home. She was getting better." Ever since Hannah had been diagnosed with cancer, she had thought of death as a monster hovering over her shoulder ready to attack at any moment. Now she realized she had not truly believed death would strike at her or any of her friends. The thought of a world without Lucy—Lucy *dead*—did not make any sense. It was as though her mother had told her the moon had disappeared.

"Lucy's cancer had spread, and none of the treatments they tried were helping anymore. She was at home because her parents didn't want her to die in the hospital." Hannah's mother paused. "But I didn't know that until this afternoon either."

"I don't want Lucy to be dead." Hannah knew she sounded childish, but she didn't care.

Her mother leaned over and kissed her forehead. "I know," she said. "I love you."

May 24

Lucy is dead. That still doesn't feel possible. I wish I could cry. Instead I just feel frozen, like the chemo dried up my heart. I can't even miss her because I don't believe she's really dead. She's just at home, with her family, like we all want to be, probably coming in for her next chemo in a few weeks.

"I want you to draw whatever you feel like," Rachel said.

At a table in Rachel's office, Hannah and Tori sat across from each other with sheets of paper, paintbrushes, and open jars of paint scattered in front of them. Tori picked up a paintbrush and pulled the jar of black paint toward her.

"Is this because of Lucy?" Hannah asked Rachel.

"It's because you have been through a lot. Lucy dying is only part of it. Art can help us tap into what we are really feeling. Then we can deal with those feelings and start to take control of them. That gives us more control over our own lives, as well."

Hannah spread a swirl of dark blue paint onto the paper. "I can't draw."

"That doesn't matter," Rachel said. "This isn't about producing museum-quality art, it's about helping you try to make sense out of your emotions. Just paint anything you want, and don't think about how it looks."

Hannah added a dark green swirl. "Why did Lucy have to die?"

"Because she was too good," Tori said bitterly. "That's what Wicky said to that nurse Gladys yesterday. She said, 'Lucy was the sweetest, bravest girl I've ever met. She was so strong. She never complained. It's true what they say about only the good dying young.'" Tori's voice rose into a high-pitched mimic.

"I liked Lucy." Hannah leaned over and dipped her brush into the black paint in front of Tori.

"Well, of course," Tori said. "I liked Lucy, too, but that doesn't mean she was perfect. She complained just as much as the rest of us. She made fun of Wicky with us. She cried when she had spinals. And I can't believe she died *because* she was nice. What would that say about the world?" A tear splashed onto her paper.

"She died because she was sick, not because she was nice." Hannah picked up a small, pointy paintbrush and dipped it into the yellow paint.

"You are all strong," Rachel said. "Cancer attacked your bodies and upset your lives, but instead of curling up and waiting to die, you have put up with treatments and found ways to be happy and have fun even in the middle of the worst thing you have ever experienced. Lucy was strong, too, and she didn't die because she was too good to live or because she didn't fight hard enough or anything like that. She died because she was sick, like Hannah said. And yes, you are sick, too, but you are both a long way from death right now. Your job at this point is to have your chemo and do what the doctors tell you—and for you, Hannah, to work hard at your physical therapy—but most of all for both of you to keep finding joy in your lives."

Tori put down her paintbrush. "I try to pretend I like death," she said in a low voice, "but actually I'm really scared."

Hannah looked at Tori's painting. It showed a graveyard at night. The closest headstone said simply, "Lucy," and under that, "A good friend." A large, silvery teardrop hung in the bottom corner.

Hannah glanced down at her own paper. Tiny yellow flowers floated on the paper, while dark storm clouds wrapped around them, encircling and threatening them. At first she thought it looked like a very depressing picture, but then she thought about what Rachel had said about finding joy. She thought that even though the storms looked like they were closing in on the flowers, the flowers were still yellow and beautiful. Maybe that was hopeful.

When Times Are Extra Tough

Sometimes it may seem as though there will never be an end to the doctor's appointments, tests, and treatments. Sometimes one can feel so depressed that nothing seems worth the effort. There are some things one can do when there seems to be no light at the end of the tunnel.

First, if one feels suicidal, help is needed immediately. Contact a mental health professional, talk to a parent, talk to a friend.

Many people undergoing difficult times for whatever reason often find it helpful to keep a journal

Depression is a concern in cancer patients, as the constant tests, treatments, and side effects can combine to make it seem as though life is not worth living. Tell someone immediately if you begin to feel this way.

where they write down anything that comes to mind. Others write poetry or paint, draw, or sculpt.

The Internet is a great resource for contacting others in cancer treatment. E-mail lists, chat rooms, and bulletin boards are all places one can look for online support groups. Always remember, though, that not everyone is who they seem on the Internet. Don't give out personal information such as your telephone number or address unless you are positively sure to whom you are giving it.

Most hospitals that treat teens with cancer run support groups or can put one in touch with a group. As with Internet support groups, it can be very beneficial to talk with others dealing with the same issue, to be reassured that one is not alone.

Art Therapy

The premise behind art therapy—using a young patient's art for a psychotherapeutic purpose—is that creating pictures allows children and young adults to express what is uppermost in their minds more genuinely and spontaneously than they are apt to do in a verbal discussion with the therapist.

The art these young patients and children of patients create is "a window into the less-conscious mind," said Estela A. Beale, M.D., a child and adult psychiatrist and associate professor in the Department of Neuro-Oncology at The University of Texas M. D. Anderson Cancer Center.

Pictures help the therapist understand the patients' feelings about what is happening to them and explore possible alternatives to solving problems. Sometimes the art expresses this information in obvious ways, but often the young artist's thoughts and feelings are "concealed, disguised, or expressed metaphorically," Dr. Beale said on a Web site called OncoLog.

For example, one young patient drew a picture of someone parachuting from an airplane over water that is full of triangles. "Oh, why is he jumping?" Dr. Beale asked.

"He's jumping because the plane is on fire and about to explode," the child told her. Beneath the man is an island surrounded by sharks—the triangles. There is also a boat in the water, but it

Talking with other people who have been through, or are going through cancer treatment can be helpful to an adolescent with cancer. Check with your medical team for web sites they recommend for online suport groups.

is empty. "Because of his illness, this child sees his life as threatened, and there is nowhere to turn for solace, encouragement, or hope," was Dr. Beale's interpretation.

Some children are unable to talk about how they are feeling, but can create art that expresses what they cannot say. An art therapist can interpret the artwork and use it to help the child identify her own emotions.

Some children are able to talk about the feelings that inspired their artwork, but others become even more frightened once they put their fears into the pictures, Dr. Beale said. To counteract this, she often keeps the discussion confined to the picture's metaphor. The children then, in their own time, work on the new ideas and concepts she presents to them, until they feel more comfortable with their condition and with the questions and fears that they experience. To the child who drew the burning plane and circling sharks, for example, Dr. Beale would not say, "Oh, the plane is not going to burn down, and you don't have to worry. We're going to erase the fire," because that would not address the child's terror. The plane, which is burning or disintegrating, clearly has something to do with the child's body, Dr. Beale said, and he wants to get away from it. Instead, she would help the child to construct alternative solutions, such as finding safety for the man with the parachute.

"Sometimes in life we feel that we are surrounded with danger," she might tell the young patient. "I imagine you feel that way when you are hurting and have to come back for chemotherapy and don't know if you are going to be able to get out of this."

Some young patients are more willing to talk about their feelings than others. Some teens and children may need help identifying their emotions. "You are very frightened," Dr. Beale might ask in that case. "What would help you?" They could then discuss, among other solutions, how the child's parents could help.

According to Dr. Beale, the way children respond to a discussion of their illness is determined in large part by how their parents talk to them about cancer. Parents who are very open about sharing information have children who are very open about their illness, their perceptions, and their fears. But if the parent is too overwhelmed by her own experience of having a child with cancer, the young person is likely to be timid about discussing his disease. Children and teens often pick up on adults' unspoken rules about what can be discussed and what can't. When this happens to a young person with cancer, he is likely to avoid any direct mention of his disease and his feelings

Parents of a child with cancer should help her find a way to talk about her illness and emotions, whether it is through art therapy, a support group, or with them.

about it. For someone like this, art therapy can be particularly helpful.

Dr. Beale described another patient who drew a picture of a house that seemed to be floating off the ground. Her parents had told her very little about her illness; the girl knew she was very ill, but she had no clear information about what was happening to her body. "She was up in the air," Dr. Beale said.

Usually, according to Dr. Beale, houses in children's drawings represent the body, which contains life. This girl's picture showed a primitive-looking house that was empty. "This house is not on the ground, is it?" Dr. Beale asked her.

"No, this house is floating. It's very light, and the people in the house like to float," the girl responded.

"But you know, this is a house that looks sad," Dr. Beale observed.

"Yes, because all the neighbors are in another city."

"That must be so lonesome, and I'm sure you know about that."

The girl was then able to discuss her own feelings of loneliness with Dr. Beale. The therapist also helped her to understand what was happening to her, which helped to allay her anxiety and reassure her.

Some parents believe they are protecting their children by not discussing their illness. In reality, however, children and teens have tremendous strength for confronting their disease—but they are stronger when they can confront it in an atmosphere of loving and understanding honesty.

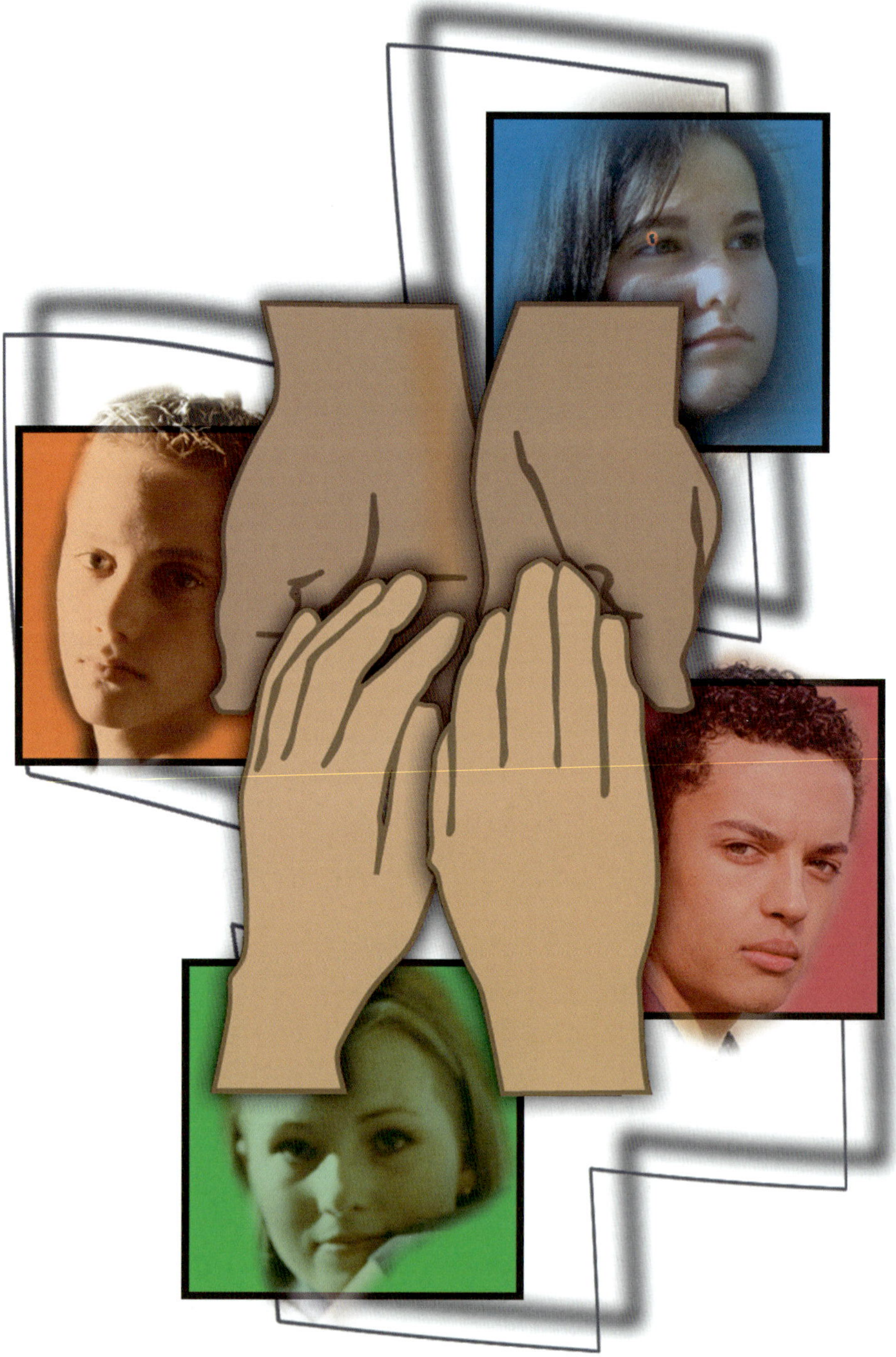

Chapter 8

The Best Party

"We may have found something on your leg scan," Dr. Stratton had said.

Those were the words Hannah had dreaded for months. She felt sick and sweaty and feverish. Was this how Terry Fox had felt—how Lucy had felt—when they heard their cancer had spread? She had almost finished the chemo. In another month, the doctors were supposed to send her on her way to happily live a long and cancer-free life.

She was at home now, curled in a ball on the living room couch with a quilt wrapped around her. Isabel was sprawled on the floor watching a movie on TV. Maddie sat in a chair, half doing her homework, half watching the movie. They didn't know yet about the results of the scan. Their mother was on the phone in the kitchen. Hannah could hear the low murmur of her voice behind the noise of the TV, but she couldn't tell what she was saying. Was she calling Uncle James and Aunt Cara to tell them the bad news?

Tomorrow morning, Hannah would have another test to determine whether the cancer had come back. Dr. Stratton had told her months ago that sometimes osteosarcoma recurred in the same place it had been removed.

Her mother walked back into the room and sat down on the floor next to Hannah. She was thinner than she had been a year ago, and her hair was pulled back into a ponytail. "Isabel," she said, "turn off the TV for a few minutes; I want to talk to you all."

Isabel immediately sat up and hit the power button on the remote. Maddie put down her book and looked up. Hannah could tell by their faces that they expected what their mother was about to say.

"We don't know for sure that the cancer has come back," their mother said, answering the unspoken question. "What we do know is that something unusual did show up on the scan Hannah had yesterday."

"But Hannah's supposed to be almost better now," Isabel said.

"Cancer is hardly ever a simple disease," their mother said. "It's tricky and complicated. But even if the cancer did come back, it's not the end of the world. Yes, we're all tired of dealing with it—especially Hannah, of course—but it would just mean we'd have to keep on fighting it a little longer."

"What will you do about your job if it is cancer?" Maddie asked. Their mother had taken the spring semester off and now, at the start of the fall semester, was teaching a much-reduced course load. The college dean had been very patient and understanding, but they all knew their mother worried about how far his patience would stretch. Not to mention that less work meant less pay.

"We'll deal with it," their mother said. "That's not something any of you need to think about. We have health insurance for the medical bills, and if we start really running low on money, James and Cara have offered to help out some. Whatever happens, we're going to be okay. We'll get through this."

Hannah lay on the exam table, waiting for the doctor to stick a needle in her leg and figure out whether that shadow on the scan really was osteosarcoma. Her mother rubbed Hannah's shoulders to relax her, and she closed her eyes. She tried to pretend she was somewhere else. A warm beach sounded good. She tried to turn the rhythmic pulsing of some piece of medical equipment into the sound of the waves hitting the shore.

No matter how many scans and tests she had, they never exactly got routine. She always had a little flame of fear inside, a tiny voice that whispered about death and the scariest word in the cancer vocabulary—*metastasizing*. This test was even worse, of course, because the doctors had already found *something*, which was bad. She didn't even dare to hope the *something* might be *nothing*, just a shadow, a glitch, a problem in the scanning machine. At the same time, she couldn't let herself think about cancer cells spreading throughout her body. She thought firmly about warm sand, light salty ocean breezes, the call of seagulls far above her.

When the needle went in, she tried to imagine she was being bitten by a snapping turtle, which somehow was more cheerful than the truth. Still, she could feel tears leaking out from under her closed eyelids and running down her face, into her ears.

She didn't know how long it had been before she heard Dr. Stratton's voice. "Sit up, Hannah," he said. "I have good news."

September 1

IT'S NOT CANCER!!! Just an infection! One of those stupid pockets of infection they told me about once, a long time ago before they did the surgery. Infection was one of the risks of the artificial knee. But this infection isn't even that bad and they just drained it and put me on antibi-

otics and I should be FINE! Better than fine. It set back my chemo schedule by a couple of weeks, but that's it and the cancer didn't spread and everything looks good!! I'm so happy I would jump up and down if I could! I can walk now, but still no jumping.

Streamers and balloons decorated the activity room. Two banners hung along one wall. One read, "Happy Birthday!" and the other, "Happy End-of-Chemo!" A huge cake sat on a table in the middle of the room. "Congratulations, Hannah!" was written in icing across the cake, and then under it, "14 years old and no more chemo!"

Hannah looked at her family and friends, and then she laughed. Her mother, Maddie, and Isabel were there, of course, and so were Uncle James and Aunt Cara. Tori and Andrew and Henry were there. Becca was there, and so was Jess. Many of the other patients and their families were there, along with Rachel and the doctors and nurses. She felt much more tolerant of the Brian Callahan for whom the activity room was named, now that she too was on the other side of a year of chemo.

"I'm happy for you, Hannah," Mandy Wickstrom said. "Now keep growing up and make us here at Pickering proud of you."

Hannah wasn't sure what she meant by that exactly, but today she even felt fond of Wicky. She smiled, thinking about her last birthday party, a year ago in the same hospital, just down the hall. Then, she was scared and didn't know what was going to happen. She still didn't really know what would happen, of course, but that was just life. She would have to come back for regular checkups, to make sure the cancer hadn't suddenly turned up again. Sometime down the road, she would probably have to have another surgery to adjust her knee implant, or even to replace it if it started having problems.

Last year, she could not have imagined being where she was today. She was a different person now than she was then. She was bald and had a fake knee, for one thing, but that was only what had happened to her body, and now that she was done with chemo, her hair would finally start growing back. A year ago, she would never have thought Dani and Lauren would stop being her friends. A year ago, she would have been afraid of Tori, who usually dressed head to foot in black, and often wore black eyeliner and lipstick, as well. A year ago, she couldn't have imagined she would make a good friend and have her die, all in a few months.

She thought of the last year as a kind of marathon, like swimming the English Channel or running across Canada as Terry Fox had tried to do. She had read a book once about a woman who had swum the English Channel; even though the woman was the one who had been swimming, people had traveled next to her in boats, shouting encouragement and making sure she was okay. Hannah imagined her mother and sisters in one of the boats, along with Uncle James and Aunt Cara. In another boat would be Becca and Rachel and the doctors and nurses. Nearby would be Tori, who was making her own voyage across the Channel. The woman in the book had said that life had looked different after she had finished the swim.

Hannah understood that now.

Helping Friends with Cancer

Before someone can help a friend with cancer, she has to know how she herself feels about the situation. It's all right to be anxious about how to interact with the friend. It's even okay to be angry that a friend has cancer. But, that shouldn't let her stay away if she is really a friend.

Friends can help each other by becoming educated about cancer. The ones without cancer can search

Once a teen is diagnosed with cancer, she may seem like a totally different person, but she is not. The best thing that friends can do for her is to treat her as they always have.

the Internet and ask teachers and other adults about cancer. There is a lot of information available about specific cancers as well as cancer in general. The friend with cancer can help others feel comfortable by answering questions, but only as much as he feels comfortable.

Most important, everyone should realize that the person with cancer just has an illness—yes, a very serious one, but an illness nonetheless—and is still the person who was a friend before he got sick. At times he may not seem like the same person, but beyond the cancer he truly is. He needs to be treated as a friend, not as someone with cancer. His treatment team is treating his cancer; what he needs from others is friendship.

Glossary

adjunct: Something added to something else.

arduous: Requiring hard work or continuous strenuous effort.

benign: Noncancerous; causing no harm.

cancer cluster: A group of cancer cases occurring within a specified area that are greater in number than might be expected.

catalyst: Something that causes an action to occur.

catheter: A thin, flexible tube that is inserted into a part of the body to inject or drain away fluid, or to keep a passageway open.

chronic: Long-term or recurring.

DNA: The molecule in which an organism's genetic information is carried.

epitomizes: Serves as a highly representative example of something.

genetics: Relating to genes, the basic units capable of transmitting characteristics that pass from generation to generation.

graft: A piece of living tissue or an organ that is transplanted to a part of a patient's body.

hormones: Chemical substances that exert regulatory or stimulatory effects.

intravenously: Provided by administration through a vein.

lesions: Wounds.

mortality: The state of being certain to die eventually.

oncology: The branch of medicine that deals with the study of cancer.

palliative care: Treatment geared toward alleviating symptoms without eliminating their cause.

pathologist: A scientist who specializes in identifying the nature, origin, progress, and cause of disease, especially one who determines the cause of a person's death through an autopsy.

predisposition: A susceptibility to a disease based on hereditary or other factors.

premenopausal: Used to describe the stage of a woman's life just before the onset of menopause.

prognosis: Outcome.

prostheses: Artificial limbs.

protocol: A detailed treatment plan.

residency: A period of specialized training in clinical medicine or surgery in a hospital on completion of an internship.

salvage: Save.

socioeconomic: Involving both economic and social factors.

triathlete: Someone who competes in an athletic contest involving three events, usually swimming, cycling, and running.

Further Reading

Alagna, Magdalena. *Everything You Need to Know About Chemotherapy*. New York: Rosen, 2001.

Cook, Hugh. *Cancer Patient*. Morrisville, N.C.: Lulu, 2005.

Fullbright, Colleen Dolan. *Cancer: How Friends Can Help*. United States: Clear River Press, 2005.

Gravelle, Karen, and Bertram A. John. *Teenagers Face to Face With Cancer*. Lincoln, Neb.: iUniverse, 2000.

Lamb, Kirsten, and Wendy Lamb. *Cancer*. Chicago, Ill.: Raintree, 2002.

Massari, Francesca. *Everything You Need to Know About Cancer*. New York: Rosen, 2001.

Rocha, Toni L. *Coping When Someone in Your Family Has Cancer*. New York: Rosen, 2000.

Thompson, John. *Lance Armstrong: Professional Cyclist*. New York: Chelsea House, 2001.

Yount, Lisa. *Cancer*. Farmington Hills, Mich.: Thomson Gale, 2000.

For More Information

American Cancer Society
www.cancer.org/docroot/home/index.asp

Candlelighters
www.candlelighters.org/justforteens.stm

Group Loop
www.grouploop.org/default_flash.php

The Lance Armstrong Foundation
www.livestrong.org

Look Good . . . Feel Better
www.lookgoodfeelbetter.org

Sloan-Kettering—For Teens Only
www.mskcc.org/mskcc/html/3335.cfm

Teens Living With Cancer
www.teenslivingwithcancer.org

The Terry Fox Foundation
www.terryfoxrun.org

Publisher's note:
The Web sites listed on this page were active at the time of publication. The publisher is not responsible for Web sites that have changed their addresses or discontinued operation since the date of publication. The publisher will review and update the Web-site list upon each reprint.

Bibliography

American Cancer Society. "The Emotional Impact of a Cancer Diagnosis." http://www.cancer.org/docroot/MBC/content/MBC_4_1X_The_Emotional_Impact_of_A_Cancer_Diagnosis.asp?sitearea=MBC.

Liddane, Lisa. "Young Adults and Teens Face Unique Challenges in the Detection of and Battle Against Cancer." *Orange County Register* (Santa Ana, Calif.), May 1, 2003.

Mayo Clinic. "Coping With a Cancer Diagnosis: Action Plan." http://www.mayoclinic.com/health/cancer-diagnosis/HQ01306.

McCollum, Sean. "Teens and Cancer: Cancer Strikes More Than 12,000 Kids and Teenagers a Year." *Scholastic Choices*, February 1, 2003.

"Parents of Children With Cancer Suffer Post-Traumatic Stress Symptoms During Treatment and Years Later." *PR Newswire*, December 13, 2005.

"Teens. Talk. Cancer. Online." *Business Wire*, February 4, 2004.

"Teens Unaware Cosmetics Are Linked to Cancer." *Palm Beach Post*, December 14, 2005.

Zebrack, Brad J., and Mark Chesler. "Health-Related Worries, Self Image, and Life Outlooks of Long-Term Survivors of Childhood Cancer." *Health and Social Work*, November 11, 2001.

Index

acute lymphocytic leukemia (ALL) 59, 60, 63
acute myelogenous leukemia (AML) 59, 60
Armstrong, Lance 64, 65, 66
art therapy 104–109

Ben's Game 67
biological therapy
  definition 79
  side effects 79
biopsy 25, 26, 30, 32, 33, 62
bone cancer 60, 61, 62
bone marrow transplant 59
breast cancer 18, 21, 78, 79

cancer
  contracting 16–23
  coping with 89–95, 103–109
  and diet 21
  and environment 21–23
  friends with 118–119
  and lifestyle 18–23
  nonmedical treatment of 48-49
  reducing risk of 23
  surgery 75
  survival 36
  symptoms 31-34
  treatment 75-79
  types 59-63
chemotherapy
  definition 75–76
  side effects 76–77
cigarettes 18, 20
cosmetics 35

Dalai Lama 67
depression 48, 103
DNA 16, 18, 19
Duskin, Ben 66–67

Ewing's sarcoma, 36, 62
exercise 88

Hodgkin's disease 36, 62, 64
hormone therapy
  definition 78
  side effects 79

Internet 104

Johnston, Eric 66–67

leukemia
  cure rate 60
  definition 59
  symptoms 59
  treatment 59
  types 59
LiveStrong 66
  wristbands 66
Look Good...Feel Better for Teens 90
LucasArts 66
LucasFilms 66
lymphoma
  cure rate 63
  definition 62

symptoms 62
treatment 62
types 63

Make-a-Wish Foundation 66, 67
moles, 31, 33

oncology 39, 43, 46, 54, 55, 104
osteosarcoma
amputation 61
definition 60
symptoms 60
treatment 60

radiation
definition 77
implants 77
side effects 77–78

smoking 18, 21
suicide 103
sunscreen 18

tobacco 18, 21
treatment
coping with 89–90, 92–95
side effects 76, 78, 79
success 75
types 75–79
tumors
appearance 16, 17
benign 32, 33
cause 16
malignant 32, 33

Watson, Barry 63, 64

Picture Credits

Artville-Getty Images: p 19
- Boyajian, Ann: p. 103
- Teebken, Tim: p. 91
- Zador, Lisa: p. 106

Corbis: pp. 33, 63
Image Source: p. 118
Jupiter Images: pp. 47, 65, 67, 89, 92, 94, 105, 108
PhotoAlto: Sheandell O'Carroll, Patrick: p. 20
Photodisc, Inc: pp. 22, 31, 77
Thinkstock LLC: p. 34

To the best knowledge of the publisher, all other images are in the public domain. If any image has been inadvertently uncredited, please notify Harding House Publishing Service, Vestal, New York 13850, so that rectification can be made for future printings.

Authors

Sheila Nelson is a freelance writer, the author of nearly two dozen educational books for children and young adults. She lives just outside Rochester, New York, with her family.

Ida Walker is a graduate of the University of Northern Iowa in Cedar Falls, and has done graduate work at Syracuse University. The author of many nonfiction books for young adults, she lives in Upstate New York.

Series Consultants

Dr. Bridgemohan is an Assistant Professor in Pediatrics at Harvard Medical School and is a Board Certified Developmental-Behavioral Pediatrician on staff in the Developmental Medicine Center at Children's Hospital, Boston. She specializes in assessment and treatment of autism and developmental disorders in young children. Her clinical practice includes children and youth with autism, developmental language disorders, global delays, mental retardation, attentional and learning disorders, anxiety and depression. Dr. Bridgemohan is Co-director of residency training in Child Development at Children's Hospital, Boston, and is co-editor of "Bright Futures Case Studies for Primary Care Clinicians: Child Development and Behavior," a curriculum used nationwide in Pediatric Residency training programs. Dr. Bridgemohan has also published research and review articles on resident education, toilet training, autism screening and medical evaluation of children with developmental disorders.

Cindy Croft, M.A.Ed., is the Director of the Center for Inclusive Child Care (CICC) at Concordia University, St. Paul, MN. The CICC is a comprehensive resource network for promoting and supporting inclusive early childhood and school-age programs and providers with Project EXCEPTIONAL training and consultation, and other resources at www.inclusivechildcare.org. In addition to working with the CICC, Ms. Croft is faculty at Concordia University and Minneapolis Community and Technical College.